Human-Centred Education

Human-Centred Education (HCE) radically rethinks the aims of education, the nature of learning, and the relationship between individuals in schools. This accessible guide presents a HCE approach to schooling and includes a variety of rich pedagogical examples. It provides practical suggestions as to how the approach might be adopted as a whole-school initiative, or else woven into particular aspects of existing school life, including the curriculum, classroom culture and feedback for learning. This handbook also illustrates how holistic educational practices, found in some alternative schools, can be introduced fruitfully into the state educational system with step-by-step guidance on how to integrate HCE into teacher training and school governance.

HCE is more than a set of inflexible pedagogical prescriptions or a recipe of lesson plans. It originates from the fundamental values of care, positive relationships and well-being. National education policies tend to ignore deeper educational processes, such as the cultivation of qualities that are central to living meaningfully and well, because they focus on measured, high-stakes academic performance. HCE is an effective antidote to this, and brings to the fore a more human-centred approach without sacrificing academic standards.

Current secondary teachers, members of school management and leadership teams, as well as those currently undertaking teacher training will all benefit from reading this important book.

Scherto Gill is a Research Fellow at the Guerrand-Hermès Foundation for Peace, and Visiting Research Fellow at the University of Sussex, Brighton, UK.

Garrett Thomson is Chief Executive Officer of the Guerrand-Hermès Foundation for Peace and Professor of Philosophy at the College of Wooster, USA.

Human-Centred Education

A practical handbook and guide

Scherto Gill and Garrett Thomson

Routledge
Taylor & Francis Group

LONDON AND NEW YORK

First published 2017
by Routledge
2 Park Square, Milton Park, Abingdon, Oxon OX14 4RN

and by Routledge
711 Third Avenue, New York, NY 10017

Routledge is an imprint of the Taylor & Francis Group, an informa business

British Library Cataloguing in Publication Data
A catalogue record for this book is available from the British Library

Library of Congress Cataloging in Publication Data
A catalog record for this book has been requested

ISBN: 978-1-138-21082-0 (hbk)
ISBN: 978-1-138-21083-7 (pbk)
ISBN: 978-1-315-45421-4 (ebk)

Typeset in Sabon
by Swales & Willis Ltd, Exeter, Devon, UK

Printed and bound in Great Britain by
TJ International Ltd, Padstow, Cornwall

Contents

Boxes

Tables

Introduction

In this handbook, we present an approach to schooling that radically rethinks the aims of education, the nature of learning and the relationships between individuals in schools. We call this approach 'human-centred education', a vision that places the human being at the heart of all educative processes.

Human-centred education (HCE) respects the person as a whole, and values the holistic growth of the individual. It focuses on empowering young people to live rich, meaningful and flourishing lives both at school and throughout their adult lives. It nurtures students' personal qualities and dispositions, such as their inner integrity and relationships with others and the world at large.

Human-centred learners are emotionally engaged, independent, knowledgeable, resourceful, insightful, creative, inquisitive, open-minded, caring young people, committed to and prepared for shaping a flourishing future for themselves and for the world around them. These are amongst the qualities that education ought to nurture in the students.

Throughout this handbook, we offer you, a teacher or school leader, the opportunity to see what a human-centred approach to education might mean in practice. It can be adopted as a whole-school initiative, or alternatively, the approach may be integrated into particular aspects of a school's life, for example, informing curriculum, pedagogy, classroom culture, and learning feedback and review.

Taking a human-centred approach does not require that a school abandon public exams, nor that teachers work longer hours. It is a systemic change that comes about when we reconceptualise education from a human perspective, and care for the development of the person as a whole. Once this fundamental shift in our conception has taken place, the rest will follow naturally.

The HCE team at the Guerrand-Hermès Foundation for Peace (GHFP, www.ghfp. org) is here to provide ongoing support and consultation for schools and learning centres, and offer in-school training and residential training in different countries.

Background

The idea of HCE arose from nearly two decades of work at the GHFP. During this time, the GHFP supported educational projects and schools worldwide, organised international conferences and symposia and conducted research in education. From these various experiences, the GHFP team asked itself: 'How can good holistic educational practices found in some alternative schools be introduced fruitfully into the state educational system?'

This question seemed particularly pertinent regarding state secondary schools. The current worldwide mainstream secondary systems are predominantly oriented towards exams, grades and measurable results, sometimes at the cost of deeper educational processes. Young people are often unhappy at middle and high schools, where childhood ends rather abruptly. At the same time, they are going through huge personal changes, which could be an opportunity for genuine transformation. For these reasons, we felt that it would be more beneficial and challenging to direct our question specifically towards secondary schooling of children between the ages of 14 and 18. In answer to the question above, we launched a research into young people's experiences in English secondary schools and summarised the insights in *Rethinking Secondary Education: A Human-Centred Approach*, which was published by Pearson Education in 2012 (Gill and Thomson, 2012).

Whilst working on the ideas, values and concerns that ideally *ought* to motivate a secondary educational system, we found that the phrase 'human-centred education' captured the essential meanings central to our thought and the innovative practices that we had observed.

Structure of this handbook

We wrote this handbook to help individuals and institutions put into practice the kind of educational vision advanced in *Rethinking Secondary Education*, which derives from the values of care, relationship and well-being. We believe that state-run education at secondary level can become more human-centred without sacrificing academic standards, and this handbook suggests practical ideas for how this can be achieved.

Unlike some school-based innovations, HCE is more than a set of inflexible pedagogical prescriptions or a recipe of lesson plans. As we will illustrate later, the handbook represents some rich pedagogical insights, including practical suggestions for institutional pathways.

Since in some regards the human-centred vision of education that we have developed is relatively new, we will present a brief outline of the theoretical grounding which underpins our approach in the first chapter. In the rest of the handbook, we attempt to show how the new theory impinges on and transforms practice.

The handbook is divided into eight chapters:

Chapter 1: Introduction to human-centred education
Chapter 2: Nurturing learning communities
Chapter 3: A framework for a human-centred curriculum
Chapter 4: Human-centred pedagogy
Chapter 5: Human-centred approach to educational evaluation
Chapter 6: Becoming a human-centred educator
Chapter 7: Educational governance
Chapter 8: Integrating human-centred education
Appendices: Further resources

Although our focus has been primarily on the English secondary education system, we believe that the practices described in this handbook are applicable to other contexts. This is because they concern the principles upon which education should be founded.

It is important for the reader to understand that HCE is a vision for a state secondary system as a whole. We are well aware that a school may find it difficult to put into practice fully the human-centred approach when the national or regional policy environment is hostile to any attempt to divert the focus away from exams and grades. Therefore, the handbook shows how to adapt HCE ideas to this kind of institutional context as far as possible given that the system isn't human-centred. Readers who are interested in pursuing HCE practices might wish to consult our website, http: //humancentrededucation.org.

At the same time, we hope that those who support HCE values and approaches will engage in national politics by advocating for policies that are more equitable and centred on the needs of young people. Without sufficient budget allocation, it is impossible to make HCE accessible to the wider society. Indeed, the more disadvantaged the children and young people, the more pressing the need for HCE. As we will discuss in Chapter 5 of this handbook and in greater depth in *Rethinking Secondary Education*, narrowly focusing on preparing for and passing exams is an impoverished educational model that does not serve our young people's needs nor support their development. By focusing almost exclusively on measured academic excellence, national policies usually ignore deeper educational processes, such as the cultivation of qualities that are central to living meaningfully and well.

Chapter 1

Introduction to human-centred education

Overview

In this chapter, we will explain briefly the core principles of human-centred education (HCE). We will preview

- the main ideas of human-centred education;
- the nature of a human-centred learning community;
- the human-centred approach to curriculum;
- human-centred pedagogy;
- learning feedback and review (instead of assessment);
- implementing human-centred education in schools.

These headings are used to organise the handbook so that school leaders, teachers, parents and students can understand the vision and ethos of HCE and acquire the know-how to apply such principles in their day-to-day practices within a school. Each of these distinct elements is elaborated in further practical detail in its own part of the handbook. For the moment in this first chapter, the aim is simply to present the ideas. Finally, towards the end of this chapter, we will discuss in general terms how schools might put these ideas into practice and give an overview of the implementation processes.

Some teachers will be familiar with the ideas advocated in this chapter and will be already putting into practice some of the practical proposals advanced later in the book. The idea that schools should serve the development of young persons is not new, and teachers have been helping students bloom for many years. This book, however, lays out a compelling new vision for the secondary schooling system based on principles for which we argue. In other words, we aim to articulate a well-reasoned, systemic alternative to the standard approach, which will weave together some old ideas into new patterns. For readers who are interested in the argumentation for the claims made in this introductory chapter, please see part I of *Rethinking Secondary Education* (Gill and Thomson, 2012). In this chapter, we simply explain the main conclusions concerning a human-centred approach. We won't discuss them academically. This work is a manual and not a tract.

Human-centred education: the main ideas

The idea of HCE has four main strands. The first concerns the aims of education; the second, the character of educational processes; the third, the nature of learning; and the fourth, the needs of students.

Aims

Educational activities have three general kinds of aim. Education should be geared at the following:

1   various kinds of social ends (such as economic growth);
2   academic ends (such as understanding how cells multiply);
3   the development of the individual.

The fundamental aim of education should be the *development of the person as a human being* understood in terms of her well-being and flourishing. This aim is paramount over two other general educational aims: academic and social ends. Human flourishing takes priority over the needs of socio-economic institutions and of academic standards, ultimately because such institutions and standards exist to serve human life. People have primary value amongst all other things of value, such as novels, factories, companies, cars and toys. This means that the living of life has primary intrinsic value. Other values are derivative. However, this doesn't mean that the development of the individual *always* precedes other educational aims in all circumstances. Nevertheless, it does mean that, whenever conflicts exist between the aims, the development of the person will take the lead in shaping the standards defined by other objectives.

Secondary education ought to be directed towards the development of the individual as a whole. Such holistic development typically points in two directions at once: outwardly towards caring for people, causes and things of value beyond oneself, and reflexively towards greater self-awareness and self-direction. Thus, it involves both greater engagement with the world and greater care and responsibility for oneself. 'Holistic development' includes a person's emotions and motivation and is not simply a way to perform better academically. It also means that the person's cognitive development will be contextualised as being integral to their overall growth rather than simply as a way to attain academic goals, which may make little sense to a young person.

Processes

The second strand to HCE is based on the principle that human life has primary intrinsic value and shouldn't be instrumentalised. We instrumentalise when we treat something that has intrinsic value as if it merely had instrumental value.

This is a profound mistake inherent in everyday conceptions of rationality. Normally, we think that only the goals of our activities have intrinsic value and that the means to those goals are merely instrumentally valuable. This way of thinking identifies intrinsic value with goals, and means with instrumental value. We can call this way of thinking 'instrumental rationality' or 'means–ends thinking', according to which we should always be efficient in achieving our goals by minimising the means.

This conception has a disastrous implication. It implies that we should treat all our goal-directed actions as merely instrumentally valuable in relation to our goals. Essentially, it means that all our activities are costs. Because efficiency requires that we should always reduce those costs, this implies disastrously that we should minimise our activities. Think about what this signifies for learning. According to instrumental rationality, the activity of learning is a cost that we bear for the sake of certain goals and which, as such, should be reduced to a minimum. Clearly, such a way of thinking cannot acknowledge that learning is an activity valuable for its own sake even though it has goals. It cannot recognise the value of learning for its own sake.

Through such reflections, we reach the important conclusion that this instrumental way of thinking cannot recognise the intrinsic value of learning as an activity. This conclusion can be generalised to all activities: instrumental rationality cannot recognise the intrinsic value of any goal-directed activity. This is because it mistakenly treats the goal as the sole source of value. It misunderstands the value relationship between lived processes and goals.

Unfortunately, instrumental rationality is rife in contemporary society. In education, it implies that the activity of learning only has value because of its goals. In sharp contrast, HCE rejects the claim that all values should be conceived in terms of instrumental rationality. Such a claim would instrumentalise all lived activities and processes. HCE rejects the instrumentalisation of human life. This has several implications.

First, it means that time at school is a lived human experience and is an important part of a young person's current life. As such, it is valuable as an end in itself. Adolescence is not merely a preparation for adult life. Therefore, respecting the young person as a human being implies not treating adolescence mainly as a time to prepare for joining a nation's workforce and contributing to the economy. It involves taking the lived experience of adolescents more seriously, and designing educational institutions that provide a culture and space for young people to enjoy this special time of life.

Second, it means avoiding seeing young people simply as empty vessels to be filled with knowledge in order to attain grades. Furthermore, the culture of a human-centred school will transcend interactions that are defined solely by roles. Roles are goal-defined functions. We are more than such functions and the culture of a human-centred school would recognise this. In this way, such a school would constitute a learning community, which we will explain in Chapter 2. In short, a human-centred educational culture would not be dominated by roles and ratings.

Third, human-centred educative processes will encourage the young people to take ownership of the learning or development they undertake. Such processes cannot be forced because they involve a person's sense of self, but they do need to be guided. All of this requires that the curriculum allocate sufficient time and the proper kind of space in order that young people can develop such ownership.

Thus, the HCE vision calls for an explicit shift from schools as controlled spaces for receiving instruction to schools as humanising learning communities. This vision will guide the planning, design and nurturing of learning communities, and place quality-based processes of personal development at the core of the curriculum. It transforms the nature of pedagogy and of learning feedback.

The nature of learning

A human-centred approach challenges the standard dictionary definition of learning as the acquisition of knowledge and skills. This view needs (at least) to be supplemented with the idea of learning *to be*; that is, to have qualities or non-moral virtues. These include character traits, such as the capacity to care for others and integrity, as well as qualities related to understanding such as curiosity, persistence and patience. These virtues or qualities are more than knowledge and skills; they involve caring about the right things in the right way.

We argue that knowledge and skills are only meaningful for a person's life insofar as they pertain to relevant non-moral virtues or qualities. Without the relevant virtues, knowledge and skills mean little. Consider what it is to be a historian or a biologist, a carpenter or a systems designer. In each case, the role is defined by caring about the right things in the right way; the skills and knowledge flow from those.

The same applies to being a person. Since the main aim of secondary education is to help young people self-develop, the qualities they need can be defined primarily in terms of living a flourishing human life. The virtues or qualities form part of the valuable features of our way of being. So they include the kinds of caring that are appropriate for the full range of our way of being. As beings who are self-aware, capable of rationality, who connect with others, who feel emotions, who have moral sentiments and aesthetic sensibilities – as such beings – to live well, we need to care in appropriate ways. In short, if education is to be centred on human flourishing and well-being, then its main aim will be the development of the person *as a whole,* which requires the acquisition of a host of relevant virtues or ways of caring.

As such, a human-centred approach will be directed explicitly towards the relevant qualities through processes of personal development. The idea of learning as a cultivation of qualities is already inherent in existing educational practices such as professional and vocational training. Even academic learning involves implicitly the nurturing of virtues. A scientist cares about the way experiments are designed, data is interpreted and theories are constructed. He or she cares deeply about some aspect of the natural world. Likewise, a historian will care about some period in the past and about how it should be described given documentary and other evidence. In each academic discipline, we learn to care.

The kinds of qualities or virtues that we need in academic, vocational, business and professional endeavours often overlap with those we require for everyday living. There is here, then, a huge underlying common ground and an immense synergy that characterises human-centred education. However, the fostering of qualities is often only implicit or indirect in mainstream education, and this is in part because qualities cannot easily be measured or tested. Test-driven instruction drives out mentorship.

In many educational processes in secondary schools, the nurturing of virtues is often only implicit and indirect. In the human-centred approach, we make it explicit and direct. Therefore, HCE will be designed explicitly for learning, defined (in part) as the nurturing of desirable personal qualities that are essential for a person to live a flourishing life.

Such qualities might typically include:

- being curious, inquisitive and reflective, having the motivation for inquiries and learning, and having the aptitudes and capacities to carry out investigations, to analyse and to draw meaningful conclusions from evidence. This will also include having an open mind, being able to listen to others, and to critically accept those who follow other traditions or have dissimilar lifestyles;

- caring about connecting well with other people, to love and to commit to friendship and relationships. This involves knowing how to understand other people and how to deal with their feelings of anger, fear and sadness. It also involves being able to apply ethical considerations in one's decision-making, and being willing and knowing how to contribute to the well-being of others, for instance, by being compassionate and forgiving;
- caring for things of value beyond oneself, such as social justice and the betterment of the world, and having strong commitment to truth, beauty and goodness;
- caring about thinking independently, creatively, critically and systematically, and being motivated to apply sound reasoning in formulating questions and developing ideas. This will also require being sensitive to the nuances and implications of language for the sake of both one's own thinking and communication with others;
- having strong self-understanding, including of one's own emotions, dispositions, talents and interests and being able to be self-respectful. This involves knowing how to deal with negative feelings such as anger, sadness, anxiety and uncertainty, having a joyful outlook on life, and being able to find peace in oneself.

The relevant qualities and virtues may differ between individuals because people have varied temperaments and characters. Furthermore, they may vary between cultures and societies. Also, what counts as a relevant quality will depend on the area of learning. However, this does not mean that the relevant qualities are purely subjective or merely a matter of opinion. Rather, it implies that learning as the cultivation of qualities and virtues must be an individually tailored process. It means that a 'one-size-fits-all' model of education can only provide something superficial. Thus, HCE must contain at its heart the capacity to adapt to the specific needs of the individual.

Needs of students

HCE takes into account the current needs of students. This handbook specifically concerns young people in secondary education. Responding to the needs of adolescents requires maintaining a delicate balance. During adolescence, young people tend to struggle for autonomy and a new sense of self, form close relationships with their peers, and can often drift from their parents and families. At the same time, they need to be supported, cared for and guided through a time of unprecedented physical, emotional, psychological and social change.

Below we list some key preoccupations and needs during adolescence.

- With an increased drive towards autonomy, often manifested in a rejection of authority, there comes a need for more opportunities to develop self-understanding, including an idea of one's future life.
- As they become more open to explore their inner world and to question the nature of reality, young people need spiritual guidance and experiences, as well as opportunities to explore and reflect. As they begin to think about right and wrong, they will need opportunities to discuss and debate issues, and to cultivate moral reasoning and moral agency.

- As they seek independence from their families and move towards closer peer friendships and more intimate and romantic relationships, all this indicates the need for safe and trusting spaces for discussing feelings, emotional experiences and relational issues. This is especially so when combined with an increased disposition to be emotionally vulnerable and more sensitive to emotions.
- Any tendency towards apathy will be overcome when young people learn to connect to the intrinsically valuable nature of activities, to develop appropriate appreciations and to confront challenges.
- Adolescents' cravings for excitement suggest a need for diversity in their activities, such as music, sport, arts and drama. Their tendency to experiment with things that are novel, such as drinking, taking drugs or smoking, presents the need for other channels for creativity and despair, as well as for clearer guidance.
- As adolescents' cognitive capabilities become more complex and sophisticated, they need appropriate intellectual engagement. With such engagement, they can strengthen their capacities to select and synthesise knowledge claims; they can interpret and interrogate the accuracy of such claims and the plausibility of arguments and better navigate the information-saturated media.

This list outlines some of the needs that adolescents may have. Education must be tailored to meet these needs and to provide opportunities for the young person to flourish. In Chapter 3 on the curriculum, we offer some detailed proposals in terms of how a HCE could be designed to meet these needs and support the growth of the student in a caring way.

The nature of a human-centred learning community

Taking a human-centred view of educational institutions is an opportunity for a fundamental shift away from the dehumanising mechanism of current mass schooling towards seeing schools as humanising learning communities. A human-centred learning community is underpinned by a culture of care and respect in which people treat each other as persons rather than as role occupants. As such, schools can provide a respectful culture in which individuals relate to each other in a caring way. Thus, school would become a home away from home for the student.

A human-centred learning community is driven by a collective search for betterment and a shared experience of meaningfulness. It is characterised by a shared commitment to a way of being and flourishing together. This means that the culture of the community encourages young people to care for and support each other with a common sense of direction.

A human-centred learning community also involves a close partnership with parents and others within the wider community. It values the participation of parents as being of crucial importance for the student's development. Parents themselves may also learn and grow as they participate in the life of the school community.

Communal life is itself part of real-life learning and collective self-reflection, dialogue and collaboration. Through these processes of 'lived citizenship', the young person develops a greater capacity to be responsible for their own learning. We will expand on this in Chapter 2.

The human-centred approach to curriculum

A human-centred curriculum is constructed around the overall developmental and current needs of the student. Its construction would not be based primarily on academic subjects and fixed end-results or learning outcomes, though these are not ruled out. Rather, the curriculum divides into time slots for different kinds of development. In this way, the curriculum will indicate the kind of open-ended processes that teachers facilitate, guided by relevant principles.

Such a curriculum will respect the student as a person by taking into account their current needs as a human being. It will also provide appropriate spaces for the development of the person as a whole rather than merely the academic and vocational training, and even those should be modulated towards the development of the whole person.

In order to respect the individual as a person, the curriculum will accord with the idea that young persons are responsible for their own development. Therefore, it will provide opportunities for them to find the fields and activities that fit their nature and interests. In so doing, it will encourage students to be proactive in identifying their own goals and in constructing appropriate learning plans. At the same time, the achieving of these goals will contribute significantly to the young person's overall development. It will be challenging in holistic ways. Therefore, such processes need to be guided by an adult learning mentor/tutor/adviser, called a Mentor thereafter, who has the capacity to see how the young person's development can be integrated with external standards.

The human-centred approach takes into account more directly the particular nature, talents, strengths and weaknesses of the student as a focus of the learning process. Where possible, the curriculum will be co-constructed with the student in close consultation with a Mentor and Subject Tutor. We illustrate how this could be done in Chapter 3.

To be integral, the curriculum will be constructed in terms of the development of relevant *qualities*, and not simply skills and knowledge. The development of central qualities or virtues is bound to involve the person as a whole. It will touch and transform the motivational, cognitive, social and affective aspects of the student's nature. A curriculum that focuses on the qualities and virtues of the whole person can offer a compelling learning experience in which individuals are actively engaged with what they have chosen to do and to learn. They are therefore more likely to become self-motivated, resourceful and responsible learners.

Once the individual cares effectively about (a) his or her own development, (b) about the people around him or herself and (c) about some areas of human knowledge, these cares can be translated into processes of developing the relevant sensitivities. Under such conditions, learning the pertinent skills and knowledge will be quite natural for most students.

In Chapter 3, we will give details concerning how to design a human-centred curriculum around a set of time allocations, rather than the conventional design around subject areas. In broad terms, the school week would be divided into six groups of activities:

1   *Direction Time:* These sessions are a space for the student to be guided through the process of shaping their own personalised timetable based on their individual interests and needs, identified together with a Mentor. These sessions provide the opportunity for the student to nurture ownership of their developmental process and to gain the self-understanding required to build the meta-structure of their educational experiences.

2   *Group Emotional Time:* These sessions are intended to enable young people to explore and share the emotional and relational issues arising for them in the context of a personal development framework. They are aimed at cultivating young people's capacities for caring, listening and understanding their emotions in positive ways.

3   *Cognitive Development Time:* These sessions are designed to help young people develop cognitively in the most direct way possible, without the additional requirements of a subject area. This would take the form of small tutorial sessions dedicated to the arts of reading, thinking, listening, writing and communicating.

4   *Individual Project Time:* In these sessions, each individual has time to develop his or her own project and work on issues that pertain to their planned life projection and personal interests. Such work could include a definite project that answers a specific question, a portfolio of art or essays, a business plan or various design projects. It might include work experience or simply focus on academic studies in the form of an inquiry, a long paper or a combination of the above.

5   *Specialist Subject Time/General Knowledge Time:*[1] During these periods, students engage with subject-specific material, predominantly offered through part lecture-style, part seminar-style classes. Teachers may also make use of online resources for factual content, enabling them to offer one-on-one support to more students.

6   *Exploration Time:* During this time, students are encouraged to explore beyond their current endeavours and to broaden their horizons. In consultation with their Mentor, the young person will determine the specific content of this part of the curriculum. The content will not be restricted by an academic focus.

The central key to a human-centred curriculum is *Direction Time*. This forms the apex of a triad with *Cognitive Development Time* and *Group Time*. Through the guidance of a caring and trained Mentor, the young person will be increasingly able to identify his or her strengths and weaknesses, how he or she needs to progress and what they are interested in and concerned about. This needs to be a shared diagnostic process. From this evolving diagnostic, the student will be able to co-construct programmes within the framework above for each term or semester, as well as holistic learning agreements that enable the student to move forward in a personally significant way. We will illustrate how this might be done in more detail in Chapter 3.

Human-centred pedagogy

The human-centred vision of education described thus far implies that teaching is a set of disparate activities, which requires different abilities and virtues from the teacher depending on their place in the curriculum. Some teachers will be more focused on guiding overall personal development, whilst others focus on cognitive capacities, emotional development or academic standards pertinent to a subject area. Thus, the criteria for a 'good teacher' in a human-centred school largely depend on the part of the curriculum for which he or she is responsible. A single conception of a good teacher would be inadequate to capture the range of educational processes.

Having said this, there are important commonalities and one of the most important qualities of any human-centred teacher is the capacity to develop caring relationships with students. Although this applies especially to the Mentors, it also pertains to all practitioners in the school who help students to nurture curiosity, caring attitudes and a love of learning. A human-centred teacher is at the same time a guide, facilitator, role model and a friend.

This handbook will focus on describing the work of three important posts that support the triad of pillars of human-centred education: the personal Mentor for the student, the Facilitator for group exploration and the Cognitive Coach.

The Mentor enables the student to have a personalised education. He or she helps the student forge links between the 'bigger picture' of their life and the educational processes at school. The Mentor guides the student towards the self-understanding required for the co-construction of a Learning Agreement and a personalised curriculum. This process combines a respect for individual choice with a recognition that students need guidance. Such a process will strengthen the capacity of young people to choose well for the sake of their own development. Adolescents are not always best at judging their needs and possibilities and so, choice requires guidance from a well-trained and experienced mentor. The mentoring process will help the students to internalise the standards that they need to take charge of their own development. To nurture a sense of their own development it is essential that students have the space to be themselves, as well as having the support of a trusted Mentor within the context of an ongoing relationship. This trust is not easily built and often takes time to establish and develop.

The work of the Facilitator is also of pivotal importance. Due to the holistic nature of HCE, a school will have teachers who can act like counsellors, guiding the non-cognitive development of young people. These 'teachers' are group facilitators who facilitate and guide intensive, emotional, sharing sessions. These facilitators construct confidential and safe spaces in which students can share, without feeling any pressure to do so. They lead the group sharing meetings in a way that helps the young people to understand more deeply their emotions and their relationships with others and to themselves.

The training sessions provided by the Cognitive Coach focus on enabling students to strengthen their cognitive abilities. These include the arts of reading with comprehension, listening attentively, writing well and thinking critically and strategically. These training sessions are important because they will enable the student to grow intellectually and in self-confidence in ways that will allow him or her to be more effective in other learning areas.

These conceptions of pedagogy are demanding and cannot be reduced to rules. They require personal judgement.

A final point here. To be human-centred, an educational organisation will respect the needs of teachers as well as those of students. This means providing space for the development of teachers as persons, rather than just narrowly focusing on professional training. The human-centred conception signifies that teachers will be able to find well-being through their work. We will highlight some of the ways an organisation can do this in Chapter 6.

Learning feedback and review

A human-centred approach to educational evaluation focuses on developing systems of feedback and review in order to further support students' learning and improve teaching. It challenges the use of testing as the major way to assess and measure students' learning. It is easy to reduce educational processes to a preparation for exams and tests, and hence, to a mere means of achieving better grades. There is increased pressure on students to view their time at school in this manner, too, and teachers and schools often reinforce that view. Ultimately, this is deeply self-defeating. When grades become the dominant goal, they prevent the student from connecting with the value or interesting features of what is being learned. In this way, the measurement destroys what it is supposed to measure, namely, the intrinsic value of the learning process. Such an educational system can turn learning into a chore only undertaken for a reward. It instrumentalises learning.

There are other negative implications of the focus on grades. It encourages students to make judgements of their worth and progress in comparison with their classmates, ignoring the fact that the nature of progress is that one has improved compared to one's own past. Furthermore, students often understand grades only in personal and judgemental terms, and use them to label themselves as failures.

To avoid these problems, an educational system can separate out the three main purposes of evaluating a young person's learning:

• To meet the learning needs of students.
• To satisfy the informational needs of employers and other institutions.
• To fulfil the need for public accountability.

These needs are distinct in nature, and can be addressed through separate means, rather than as one grand process called 'assessment' that attempts to serve all three purposes at once. Lumping learning feedback together with assessment in the format of exams fails to respect the person because it involves testing the students for the sake of ends that are not theirs. In this way, the system instrumentalises learning for the sake of the informational needs of external bodies.

In the current UK climate, schools have little choice about how they meet the needs of employers, institutions and public accountability – standardised testing and grading, culminating in public exams, are what is expected. They do have, however, greater scope for meeting the learning needs of students in more radically diverse ways.

We propose, therefore, that feedback on students' work and learning reviews not be regarded as 'assessment'. From a human-centred view, feedback from teachers and peers offers valuable opportunities for the students to understand their progress with regard to their own goals, as well as in accordance with external standards. Learning review also enables students to appreciate better how these standards relate to more basic epistemological values. At the same time, a human-centred approach encourages more active self-evaluation in terms of the one's own past (ipsative feedback). This approach has four very important features:

• It requires understanding the relevant standards well, i.e. what counts as good in this context.
• It embodies the idea that individuals are responsible for their own learning and promotes more proactive motivation.

- It includes critical self-reflection, an important human quality.
- It encourages students to improve relative to their own past rather than by being better than others.

If the student feels intrinsically motivated by and connected to what they are doing they are more likely to take responsibility for their own learning. Such motivation can be fostered by helping students understand the general value of schooling and the more specific value of any learning process and by involving them more directly in identifying their own trajectories in learning. Ongoing feedback enables students to reflect on their experiences and to use reflection to guide further learning. In Chapter 5, we will provide a detailed illustration of how learning feedback might help students to grow holistically. Examples will be given to show how schools can integrate such rigorous feedback in the learning process and help the learner to see their own progress over time, to understand their talents, strengths and needs, and to identify meaningful work.

Implementing human-centred education in schools

To guide a school through the process of becoming more human-centred, the nine parts of this handbook provide:

- an overall introduction to the concept of human-centred education, including its underlying values, key principles, conceptions of curriculum, pedagogy and learning feedback/review (this current chapter);
- practical guidelines on building a school as a learning community, including developing an understanding of the nature of a learning community, the part that the school's vision, ethos and policies can play in creating, nurturing and developing the community, the physical environment, and the characteristics of the community's life when actively pursuing a relational culture together (Chapter 2);
- practical guidelines on developing a human-centred school curriculum, which is qualities-based. These guidelines show how the different curricular elements interact towards supporting the students' experiences and overall development (Chapter 3);
- practical guidelines on developing the pedagogical processes and outlining the teachers' corresponding activities to support the curriculum (Chapter 4);
- practical guidelines on developing a system for student feedback and learning review, including some examples illustrating how learning can be monitored without resorting to grades and exams (Chapter 5);
- a set of ideas for developing teachers' qualities and practical suggestions for in-service teacher training and mutual learning (Chapter 6);
- a detailed outline of a human-centred approach to school governance, including the use of collaborative and co-creative ways to lead and guide the school community (Chapter 7);
- practical guidelines on shifting the school from an educational institution to a learning community, including initiating the processes necessary for the community to arrive at a shared vision and ethos, ways to develop policies for implementing human-centred education, and the practical steps that the school community needs for actively living human-centred values (Chapter 8);
- appendices charting additional resources for school and classroom use (Chapter 9).

The situation of each school is different. Some schools may feel that they would like to and can implement a human-centred model as completely or as fully as possible. Other schools may feel that their situation requires a more cautious or step-by-step approach, perhaps because of the policy climate within the country or region or because of a lack of resources.

We understand that the extent to which a school can adopt a human-centred approach will depend on its material resources, its human capacities and other factors. For these reasons, this handbook caters for three different levels of engagement:

1 *Values-based approach (minimum commitment)*: At the simplest level, implementing the human-centred approach requires systematic institutional reflection on how the school might create the conditions for student holistic growth, asking what the values and principles of HCE means for their school. At this initial level, we can provide guidelines that help an institution to understand what such a transformation would mean practically for the school.

2 *Flexible approach (intermediate commitment)*: If a school wants to put HCE into practice without engaging in major structural changes then we explain the desired changes, taking the school's existing educational framework as a given. This level of engagement allows for cumulative improvement rooted in deeper educational thinking.

3 *Holistic approach (maximum commitment)*: This approach aims at implementing HCE in all aspects of the school's practice. The handbook provides an integral vision for human-centred education, which can be integrated fully within a school community.

It is worth noting that uptake of the model for an entire school would likely require proportionally less financial investment, as the model by nature lends itself to widespread sharing of resources, both human and otherwise.

For schools interested in taking these ideas beyond the values-based approach, given the resources and training required we recommend that the school commits to implementing a human-centred approach to a single year group for a period of three years starting ideally from the cohort at the age of 14. In other words, the students in this group would receive human-centred practices over a period of three years.

The school would need to dedicate sufficient time each week to specifically designed HCE sessions for these students. This is because it is key to the human-centred approach that students have access to sufficient Direction Time to enable them to understand their development path and its educational implications. Furthermore, without sufficient time for emotional sharing and cognitive development, the whole idea of the growth of qualities could become insufficiently addressed.

At the same time, we recommend that other activities in the school reflect a broadly human-centred ethos. The reframing of what education is about is very important for the process to be successful. This reframing would need to be understood by the whole community.

The introduction of the human-centred approach into a school consists in several discrete steps with different members of the community which are outlined below (see Chapter 8 for more details).

First, the school community as a whole arrives at a common vision and ethos. This will include coming to a shared decision to implement the human-centred approach at some level of commitment. The school leadership will plan the process as a whole, including how to involve different members of the community.

Second, given consensus on the vision for the school, the school governing body or leadership team will launch a process of articulating some policies and key practices especially regarding the learning experiences of the students. This process will be ongoing and involves consultation with the teaching staff. At the same time, the community as a whole will express its ethos or culture, which illustrates the kind of relationships that the community would like to embody. This expresses how values are lived in day-to-day situations including approaches to communication, spaces for dialogue and for listening, and physical features of the school. The details of these suggested processes are described in Chapter 2.

Third, the school will need to establish a curriculum based on human-centred principles. This means that the core leadership team of the school will begin with an initial proposal as how best to implement a human-centred curriculum given the context and resources of the school. This process must be shared with the teachers. If time constraints allow, students could also be involved in this process. In Chapter 3 and Chapter 8, we recommend some guidelines for this construction process.

Fourth, the teaching team of the school would need to be introduced to the main pedagogical practices of HCE and there ought to be discussions amongst the staff on how to implement these given the resources, time constraints and commitments of the school community. It will also involve assigning specific tasks to particular individuals. There will also be a need for review and training sessions. These aspects of HCE are covered in Chapters 4, 6 and 8 of the handbook.

Finally, it is important for the school to establish good learning feedback and review processes for students. In Chapter 5, we will show how this might be done. We will assume that students will still be taking public exams from around the age of 16, and so we will trim and adjust the relevant feedback processes accordingly.

At the same time, the school team will want some evaluation of how successful the process of introducing HCE into the school has been over a three-year period, and at regular intervals during that period and consider how to make improvements to the process. This also will be introduced in Chapter 7.

Some of these suggested processes will only be relevant to schools wishing to implement HCE on a whole-school scale. Nevertheless, it will help those who are implementing HCE more minimally to understand how the full implementation would look in a human-centred school. This might provide insight concerning the ideal aspiration. In Chapter 9, there is a list of appendices providing practical resources, relevant websites, additional literature and other helpful examples on some aspects of HCE being implemented in schools worldwide.

Conclusion

We understand that the implementation of human-centred values and principles needs to be adapted to the specific circumstances of each school and community. This isn't something that can be done in a pre-packaged way. Therefore, the GHFP is committed to helping each school to engage with the ideas in a practical way given the constraints of their school. We offer a range of support for schools who are implementing a human-centred model, including telephone and email support with one of our team, running HCE training and mentoring courses, and facilitating the development of online networks enabling support and collaboration between human-centred schools.

In addition, we also create spaces for seminars and symposia to bring teachers and educators together in order to reflect on the challenges they face, as well as to examine helpful case studies that illustrate how HCE can be implemented in different settings.

Note

1 In chapter 3, these will be discussed separately.

Chapter 2

Nurturing learning communities

Overview

In this chapter, we explore the nature of a human-centred community and describe what it means to be and learn together through engaging in the life of a learning community. The five key themes of this chapter include:

- value, ethos and principles;
- physical environment;
- relational environment;
- an overall culture of care;
- leadership and governance.

A human-centred school is a *community* of learners. This idea involves a radical reframing of what a school is. This reframing is required in order for the human-centred approaches to curriculum, pedagogy and learning feedback to reinforce each other. In each case, putting the person at the centre means treating the school as a learning community. This inevitably involves rethinking a school's identity and the nature of its culture. Although this process of rethinking may vary according to the specific circumstances of each school, there are some common key issues:

a   The school will be a *community*. By this, we mean that students, staff and other stakeholders have a strong sense of 'we-ness' and belonging (Thomson *et al.*, forthcoming). Because of this, they feel a responsibility towards each other and towards the betterment of the school. In a school community, all members know and respect one another, adults and young people alike. Such mutual knowledge does not come by itself; people have to interact through community meetings, joint activities and fora.

   This idea of a community has three features important for the conception of a human-centred school.

   First, it reflects the social and relational nature of our being: our being is always already *being-with*. Human life is simultaneously material, emotional, intellectual, moral and spiritual, but it is also social and relational. So too are the diverse experiences, activities and processes that comprise it. It has intrinsic value because the person who is living the life does. We are valuable, worthy of respect and because of this, our lives and its components have value. However, if this is true of anyone then it is true of everyone. This point indicates the moral nature of being human, central to which is an acceptance of other people as moral beings who are equally worthy of our love and respect, however different they may be from ourselves. This feature of the community will be embodied in a human-centred school.

Second, humans are finite, and because of this, our worldviews are always situated in our histories, cultural practices and personal contexts. Nevertheless, we can be aware of these limitations and strive to overcome them in order to understand better. This is one central aspect of learning. But it is also a feature of relationships. When we engage with others, we need to overcome our limitations in order for the relationships to be more meaningful. Part of being in a meaningful relationship is that the views, emotions, desires and beliefs of the other person affect one's own understanding and cares. As such, our growth is enriched by others we encounter.

Third, the previous two points indicate that we are participatory subjects, which means that we live among others, in relationships with them. However, in addition we are contributive subjects, which means that we give to others and we care for them (Thomson, *et al.*, forthcoming).

Being a person involves becoming consciously aware of our existence with others in these three ways. Recognition of this is part of a human-centred definition of community. For these reasons, the self cannot be conceived as a bounded singular individual. Instead, each person is a relational being whose living is intimately connected to others.

b   The school will be a *learning community*. The members of the community are brought together by the common intention to learn and to develop holistically. Furthermore, each member of the community acknowledges that the community exists for this reason and is aware that everybody shares this same understanding. Mutual recognition of the school's aims is vitally important for the realisation of a shared culture, but it takes time for the community to build it.

When we call a school 'a *learning* community', in part this means a community in which we learn to become more fully human through our lives together in the community. Learning for its own sake is an integral aspect of being in such a community. The community is not merely a group of people who have a common instrumentalised task. It is a shared way of being together, valuable for its own sake.

This shared culture will define the values that are accepted implicitly by everyone. Paramount is that the community is permeated by the practices of care, mutual concern and respect. A culture of such relationships expresses itself as openness, a general feeling of joyfulness, friendliness and warmth.

Once the school has embraced the values of respect and care for the whole person, the school's team can strengthen the learning environments and develop appropriate approaches to teaching and learning. These approaches will focus on the flourishing of the whole person in a personalised way. This may seem like a costly endeavour, especially in a society that wants immediate and measurable results. (We will return to this important point later.) This is one reason why we stress inclusive leadership processes. All the key stakeholders need to be involved in the development of the educational vision and ethos of the school. This will include governors, staff, young people and parents. Once they are behind the vision, they can hold at bay the demand for quick measurable results.

Inclusive leadership is also important because in a human-centred learning community, each person feels empowered to contribute to the future of the school. For both students and teachers this empowerment is part of their personal development process, as well as being an important aspect of being a community.

Inclusive leadership has implications for the nature of the general culture of the school. It requires a mutual feeling of trust, which in turn needs a culture of listening and engagement. This has further implications for the members of the community: their actions build this culture. The engaging will be sensitive to diverse groups in the community such as differences of ethnicity, gender, sexual disposition, intellectual and physical ability, and socio-economic background.

In summary, a human-centred understanding invites us to re-envisage all aspects of a school, for example, its physical spaces, its overall culture and the inner environment of the individuals, as well as its educational processes and organisational structures.

It is important to stress that it is the responsibility of the school community to work out how to develop according to human-centred values. In this regard, manuals such as this can only provide guidelines that a community adapts to their unique circumstances. Our task is to make helpful suggestions, but not to prescribe specific outcomes.

Values, ethos and principles

We wrote this handbook as a practical extension of an earlier work on human-centred education (HCE) (Gill and Thomson, 2012). As we saw in Chapter 1, the first principle of HCE is that persons have primary intrinsic value, and therefore, human life should not to be instrumentalised. We also pointed out that secondary education does tend to be instrumentalised; for instance, for students, learning is often presented as a way to perform better on tests for the sake of a grade, and the whole system is conceived merely as preparation for society's workforce.

The primary principle of HCE rejects this instrumentalisation. It implies that the time at school is valuable in itself. The activities and experiences that young people engage in at school are valuable in themselves; processes of learning are intrinsically valuable. So too are the relationships that the students have with each other and with other members of the community. The challenge is how to appreciate these activities, processes and relationships as valuable in themselves. The fact that these activities are also means to other things, such as the development of the person, ought not to detract from their intrinsically valuable nature and from our capacity to appreciate that value. In other words, in accordance with the processes described in Chapter 1, we can resist the temptation to instrumentalise learning because it is useful.

The primary principle also means that as a learning community, the school is a way of being and a way of being with one another. We, as a community, engage in collective learning activities for their own sake. This intrinsic value does not deny that learning in a community is also a means to other things, such as the holistic development of the person. In fact, the more the students participate in the life of the school community, the more likely they take responsibility upon themselves and the better they will contribute to the learning and well-being of others within the community.

Let us briefly examine some of the implications of this central idea and some of the questions that arise from it.

1   Because of the primary principle, HCE emphasises that learning involves the acquisition of virtues or qualities. Generally, these qualities are appropriate ways of caring and, as such, they are not reducible to knowledge and skills. For instance, one of the qualities that HCE aims to cultivate is caring about one's own development, including one's learning processes. This means, among other things, being motivated generally to engage in activities of inquiry and exploration. It means caring about the things that one studies. However, the specific qualities or virtues will vary for different areas of study. For instance, the virtues that form an aspect of mathematics education are quite different from those pertaining to the study of literature. These points give birth to many questions about the cultivation of virtues or qualities. How can school activities encourage certain character traits or qualities? How does the school decide on the virtues and qualities that it should nourish both in general and for specific parts of the curriculum?

2   A host of other qualities or virtues follow from the human-centred principle that human lives have primary value. These virtues pertain primarily to caring for each other and to being a member of a community. HCE involves the development of these virtues because they are an integral part of human life. At the same time, a school as a learning community is characterised by the care that each member has for others. So, HCE also involves the development of these virtues because it is part of what a learning community is.

   These points invite many practical questions regarding, for example, how to strengthen the relationship and rapport between teachers and students. How can we create educational opportunities that enhance these human relationships? What kinds of curriculum and pedagogy strategies are needed?

3   The HCE principle that persons have primary intrinsic value has moral implications, as does the idea that schools are caring learning communities. As we mentioned earlier, such a school will be committed to the inclusiveness and equality of its members, regardless of their backgrounds, capabilities, preferences, interests and aspirations. This commitment to inclusiveness and equality opens up questions such as: How does the school engage with diverse members so that each person feels that he or she counts? How does the school develop the feeling of belonging? What kinds of process are necessary to develop a mutual sense of being-with or communing in the school?

4   A learning environment that cares for the student will provide learning processes that are appropriately challenging. To challenge the student, the curriculum needs to be personalised insofar as possible. This point prompts a host of questions pertaining to the school's time schedule, arrangement of physical spaces and the design of the curriculum. For instance, how does a school develop individualised timetables given its resource limitations?

5   A personalised education offers the students choices in terms of what they would like to study and how. Making choices requires that one has an understanding of the criteria involved. The more challenging educational activities are, the more guidance the student will need. Likewise, the more a curriculum provides the student with a range of choices, the more support he or she will need. This means

that the relationships between the teachers and the students are close rather than purely functional. This indicates questions concerning how to create time for nurturing such relationships and how to ground relational practices in teaching.

6   Holistic learning depends on the qualities of relationships within the community. Given this, it is important that a human-centred school provides opportunities for young people to experience emotions and that it offers support to the young people concerning those emotions. How can teachers make such spaces safe? What settings are needed for the young people to explore feelings and emotions together? How can young people learn about relationships with each other?

7   In a learning community, teachers will care for the future life of the young people. They will support students to work through different aspects of life, such as the emotional, intellectual, relational, material and spiritual. They will help them develop sound self-knowledge and a conception of what their life might be like. This will enable the young person to feel more ownership and responsibility for the future trajectory of his or her life. From such a feeling, the young person will want to understand him or herself better: What are my strengths and weaknesses? What are my talents? What are the possible trajectories of my life? The curriculum will provide space for the student to engage with these personal questions. This point urges questions such as: What opportunities can the school provide to enable students to expand their horizons and to explore different pathways? How can educational processes provide guidance so that students seek directions appropriate to themselves?

In summary, the primary principle of HCE defines associated core values such as care, engagement and responsibility. These in turn have implications for other aspects of the school, for example its general culture, its mission, the nature of leadership, the curriculum, and pedagogy, as well as the physical spaces.

Physical environment

Every learning community will emerge from the process of envisioning with a different image of how their school could be. In this section, to assist with this process we make some suggestions regarding the physical environment, ethos and relationships of a school as we understand them, to reflect the human-centred vision.

For the learning community to be a home away from home, it needs a relaxed and casual atmosphere. The physical space will be friendly, attractive and safe. This space blurs the boundaries between school and home. It includes a formal place for studying and an informal space for hanging out, that is, a leisure and cultural centre. Informal and inviting spaces can foster informal encounters between the students and staff, for instance, in the cafeteria or the library.

When starting a school, it is not easy to find the perfect premises, and for existing schools transitioning towards a human-centred model it may be even harder to make the needed physical changes. The spaces and physical features of the school environment would ideally emerge from the community's own processes, (i.e. being co-designed by the students, parents, teachers and others in the community), and each school will want a set of unique features. However, some generally desirable characteristics express human-centred values and principles.

- *Integrated in the local community*. Ideally, a human-centred learning community would be within walking distance of local businesses, community centres, residential areas and public services (e.g. hospitals, police stations). This will enable young people to more easily make links with the local community, including through work experience and visits, and raise the profile of the school in the community by its proximity.

- *Flexible teaching spaces*. The traditional classroom setting with rows of tables and chairs has long been challenged. From a human-centred perspective, the diversity of curriculum activities demands flexibility of space design, rather than a mere critique of a particular setting. Flexibility allows horseshoe-shaped classrooms, or the group sitting in a circle, both of which enable the group to meet face-to-face. It also stresses that the teacher is not at the centre of the stage but is also part of the group, although he or she is at same time the facilitator and guide in the learning process.

- *Large indoor spaces with natural light*. These spaces are particularly valuable for Group Time (see Chapter 3). Young people need spaces where they can feel free to make noise and where they can be physically more distant from one another. Too often classrooms feel crowded and controlled. Large spaces where students feel less constrained are likely to provide opportunities for more creativity and emotional development.

- *Green outdoor spaces*. These have similar benefits to the indoor spaces described above but with the advantages of fresh air and no walls! Inspiring outdoor spaces can also offer students an alternative working environment when they do not wish to study indoors, as well as opening opportunities for young people to develop their gardening and other outdoor skills, for instance, during Independent Project Time (see Chapter 3).

- *Outdoor spaces for organised sports*. Outdoor spaces for organised sports are ideally considered as part of the school's environment. The spaces can have a sufficient range of sport-specific apparatus. For schools that do not have such spaces, access to such outdoor spaces, for example, a community sports centre, sports ground and similar sports facilities, would be necessary.

- *Large and fully stocked library*. The school's library facilities need to be extensive due to the independent nature of much of the study in a human-centred school. Students need access to a wide range of materials in their own time. It is also desirable for the library to have sufficient comfortable study space close to the books where students can carry out independent study. Contemporary libraries stock more than a collection of books, journals, magazines, and so forth, where possible there could be a digital library, a visual and audio library as well as online and physical records of students' writings, arts and performances.

- *Access to technology and specialist facilities*. A human-centred school would have sufficient technological resources, such as computers, Internet-based educational resources, and so on, to enable students to access learning materials to carry out their own research. It would also support technology-based learning styles that some staff may employ. Students would also have access to specialist facilities and technology such as darkrooms, cameras, laboratories, design technology apparatus and art supplies.

- *Quiet spaces for solitary time*. There are spaces where young people and adults are able to spend time alone, to reflect, think or simply to clear their minds. Giving members of the school community the possibility of removing themselves from the often-intense social and academic environment and seeking their own company is a way of respecting them. Time spent alone can be powerful in enabling young people to be more thoughtful and less stressed, and it can help them connect with the spiritual and with nature. Both outdoor and inside spaces would make it possible for students and staff to seek solitude at any time.

In the example given below, we can see that a human-centred school environment would not separate itself from the wider local community. There are myriad spaces designated for different purposes and there is flexibility in how each space is to be used. Both purposeful design and unplanned spontaneity make the school community a rich resource for all.

Box 2.1 Bishop Park College's purposefully designed community

Bishop Park College in Clacton-on-Sea, Essex, England (2002–2012) was a tailor-designed secondary school. The design had considerable input from the students. Its environment was full of light, spacious and airy, and engendered a sense of openness and well-being. There was the intention to make the learning space humane and human in scale, and the building catered for three 'schools within the school', or mini learning communities which were connected through a central atrium.

    The boundaries between the school and the wider community were minimal. For instance, in the school's compound there was a nursery, a care home for the elderly and a public library open to all. The cafeteria was a focal point of the community where students and staff members interacted during lunchtime and over refreshment. The school's main building had many other spaces designated for informal meetings, quiet reflection and for conversations and socialising.

Through the design and structure, the physical space intends to engender a sense of community, a togetherness, or a 'we-ness', where each individual appreciates and acts on their responsibility for themselves and for the community. In this way, the school's physical environment is integral to the overall curriculum design, pedagogical intention and the needs of the students.

Relational environment

We have argued that relationships and learning are mutually supportive and closely intertwined (Gill and Thomson, 2012). On the one hand, learning occurs within the context of a set of relationships, and in a human-centred learning community, these relationships support and deepen learning processes. The student's relationship with the teacher enables his or her learning to be holistic or in other words, to be a process of personal development. At the same time, relationships themselves directly involve learning. For instance, to be in a relationship partly consists in being open to the other person. This is a form of learning. The relationship is comprised of communications and as the relationship improves, the communications do too, which again is a learning process. In HCE, this kind of learning becomes part of the general educative process of the school. It becomes less implicit. By explicitly reflecting on these relationship-based learnings, we can learn more about oneself, others and living in relationships.

However, in a human-centred school, neither relationships nor learning will be treated merely instrumentally. Educative processes are to be permeated by and grounded in genuinely caring human relationships that are not valued merely for their utility.

How is such a relational environment fostered in a school community? First, the relationships between teachers and students will be authentic. This means that both are willing to express the attitudes and feelings that they have, rather than putting on a mask designated by a particular role. It also implies that they are willing to be themselves in the relationship. In some regards, the relationship transcends the roles.

Second, people in the school need time to get to know and like each other. A culture of care implies that everyone has warm regard towards one another. This is part of respecting the other person as someone of intrinsic value. In a caring relationship, one can sense one's own worthwhileness and this can constitute fundamental support for a young person who might tend to feel undervalued. In fact, people tend to have caring relationships with each other when there are good opportunities for this to occur and when there are no obstacles in the way. This suggests that the culture of caring requires that people have time to get to know each other. Relationships cannot be rushed.

Third, we can foster a caring environment by sensitive, active and deep listening. This can bring a teacher closer to understanding his or her students. Listening is the most potent and profound ingredient in building strong relationships and a human-centred pedagogy. The more a student is empathetically listened to with respect and acceptance, the more it is possible for the student to develop a caring attitude and responsibility for him or herself. The less judgemental a teacher is the more open the students will tend to be. We will return to these points in the next section when we discuss the culture of caring within the school community.

When efforts are put into nurturing strong relationships, a student will experience the school as safe. The safety includes feeling free from fears, such as the fear of bullying, punishment, failure, being judged negatively, and of authority. This suggests that such an environment will have few systems of reward and punishment. It also means that it will be relatively free from discourses of success and failure and from authoritarian impositions on the students. In a similar vein, teachers will not be judged solely or mainly in terms of exam-defined 'success rates'.

Relationships are built on trust. Motivation by reward and punishment implies distrust. So, instead of relying on rewards and punishments to motivate actions, the school will encourage open conversations relevant to motivation, such as taking responsibility for one's own actions, the joy of learning, what motivates one's learning and what matters for the individual and the community. These conversations might happen both inside and outside of classroom settings. Moreover, systems of reward and punishment tend to be based on the exercise of power without relation to content. They encourage obedience without understanding. They instrumentalise motivation by disconnecting it from content or meaning. This point is very important concerning learning. For students to appreciate the intrinsic value of learning, they need to be motivated directly by the content of the learning. In sharp contrast, rewards and punishments encourage motivation based on purely instrumental factors that do not pertain to content.

In summary, one way of developing a culture of trust is to remove systems of reward and punishment, which will enable the students to connect better to the relevant intrinsic values. This is illustrated in the example below.

Box 2.2 Building a trusting learning community at the Bina Cita Utama School

Bina Cita Utama, a school located in central Borneo, Indonesia, features a truly relational environment. To nurture relationships and create a relational environment, the school takes a collaborative, student-centred approach to learning. The school believes that each young person must take responsibility for his/her own learning and contribute to the well-being of others and growth of the community. Thus, the students' work focuses on topics and projects of both personal and social interests identified by the students and teachers together.

Project-based learning has been particularly motivating for the students, and hence there is no need for a system of reward and punishment to motivate students extrinsically. In fact, the school sees such a system detrimental to relationships and unhelpful in enabling students to take responsibilities for the right reasons (http://www.bcuschool.com/).

In a learning community, students and adults are immersed in human-centred values which form the basis of how everyone acts together. Each person treats everyone else as a person, and in turn, each is respected as a person. In this way, in a human-centred school, everyone feels supported and there is recognition that the support of others is important in one's quest to develop one's own life and to understand the world. Within such a relational environment, students and staff experience themselves and each other as part of a community to which they have a sense of belonging.

When the relational environment is mature in this way, students will likely experience a kind of buzz or a flow, a vibrancy that comes from being in an engaged and supportive community. This energy can only arise from an appreciation of learning as non-instrumentally valuable. The other side of this is that in a strong relational environment, all members of the community recognise that they have a power. They have the capacity to influence how things are run.

An overall culture of care

Earlier we mentioned that a key to whole-person pedagogy is the teachers' care for the student. This relationship can inspire the student towards a more caring attitude towards the two aspects of their own learning. The first aspect points outward: as a learner, one connects to the meaningful aspects of what learning is about. The second points inward: one has an appreciation of one's learning journey as part of one's development, and this includes the nurturing of the character traits essential for a flourishing life.

Central to the culture of care are the close relationships between the teachers and the students. This means there is time within the school's timetable to enable teachers to get to know their students and let their students get to know them. In Chapter 3, we will discuss various ways in which this could be done as part of the human-centred curriculum. Below is an example of how a school in Colombia uses the 'home visit' as a way to get to know students and to provide care that is suited to each individual student's unique needs.

Box 2.3 Nurturing a culture of caring in the school community

Colegio Amor was founded in 1988 in a shanty town outside of Bogotá, Colombia. It caters for children and young people from displaced families who have suffered from various traumas and injustice. The school conceives love as a transforming agent which is a door to a better world. This concept of love and care is then translated into teaching, learning and community projects. The founders call this 'love in action'.

Care in the school is expressed in many ways. Here we draw one example of the home visit. The home visit is part of the school's routine and each classroom teacher visits every student's home twice a year. Through these visits, the school seeks to build a bridge between school and home lives of its students. Teachers can learn about the child's home environment including economic status, parents' psychological well-being and parent–child relations. Home visits help the school to develop an appropriate attitude and strategy to care for the students and for the school/community, and strengthen the bonds between the teacher, the student, the school and the family.

When there is care, love, trust and respect for each person's worth within the school community, education is more likely to meet students' needs and to support their processes of becoming more mature and more responsible. A young person who is educated in a culture of care will be more acutely aware of the community of which he or she is a part.

Some teacher qualities are very important for building a culture of care in a human-centred school. The first is the teacher's self-acceptance. Teachers who accept themselves will be at peace with themselves and will have nothing to prove to others. As a result, they will tend to be less judgemental of students. This quality indicates the need for teachers to have opportunities for personal development.

The second quality is the teacher's motivation to communicate with the student clearly, openly and expressively. The teacher needs to engage authentically with the student, without becoming emotionally entangled. This requires the exercise of empathetic understanding.

The third quality is the capability to remain non-judgemental but at the same time to affirm a so-called 'objective evaluation' of the student. Such a teacher can be truthful without being critical. In doing this, the teacher will tend to see the student for his or her potential, rather than as defined or limited by his or her past. This quality is needed to be able to challenge the student in ways that he or she really needs to be challenged.

In summary, a culture of care is constituted by the adults in the community proactively living out human-centred values. This occurs when these values permeate the day-to-day teaching, the micro-interactions within the community and the design of the school's educational and governance processes. This culture makes it safe for all students to feel that they belong.

Leadership and governance

What does leadership and good governance look like in a human-centred school? First, a culture that is conducive to care cannot be imposed like a set of rules. Rather, it has to be nurtured through the daily practices of the community. It needs leaders who are capable of human-centred thinking that recognises the intrinsic value of human life. Without this ethos, relationships and learning processes may quickly become instrumentalised.

In a human-centred school, governance is values-based and leadership is collaborative rather than hierarchical and authoritarian. The approach to governance embodies cohesiveness, cooperation and co-creation. It makes leadership a communal process. This means that the ethos of the school will be developed collaboratively. Such processes provide an opportunity for individuals to develop closer relationships which is a part of leading. As we shall see in Chapter 7, this means that the governors and leadership team create spaces for listening and dialogue so that diverse voices are integrated in the policies and decision-making.[1]

Second, in a human-centred learning community, leadership will prioritise mutual support and reciprocal learning among the teachers. They will foster the teachers' commitment to their work and a renewal of good practices based on HCE values. However, teacher support is not restricted to continuing professional development and it is not limited to learning more about one's subject area. It includes additionally the development and flourishing of teachers as persons. Teachers aren't slaves of the school. They are persons who want to belong to and to develop with the school. They need support to enjoy the intrinsically valuable nature of teaching and to experience the great pleasure of seeing young people grow.

Third, a key concern of human-centred governance is the young people's self-responsibility. The governing body can nurture this quality by providing opportunities for young people to dialogue about and participate in school decisions. It will include young people's voices in the design of the school community and of the curriculum.

Fourth, human-centred governance appreciates the important part that parents play in the learning community. Although adolescents may not be eager to see their parents at school, it would be less awkward if parental involvement were integral to the school from the outset. This involvement goes beyond parents being members of the governing body. It also transcends the seeking of parents' feedback on new school initiatives.

Fundamentally, parents need to be on board with the human-centred mission of the school. This support constitutes the backbone of the school.

We will return to these aspects of the school in Chapter 7 where we discuss what collaborative governance might look like in practice.

Conclusion

In this chapter, we have outlined some ideas about how to nurture a learning community.

These are proposals for policy dialogues that enable the school to become more human-centred. However, we encourage the school to examine features of school life in its own terms rather than simply following the handbook. These important aspects of school life might include classroom culture, the participation of students in the design of their learning activities, how to make learning more holistic, and how the community can become more caring and loving.

In a human-centred school, individuals will be treated as persons rather than objects. This perspective creates an opportunity for a fundamental shift away from the dehumanising mechanisms of current schooling towards a human-centred learning community. Under such conditions, individuals can relate to each other in human ways and co-create a culture of care. Often in a human-centred learning community, the closeness between all people touches and changes the individual. In the next three chapters, we will look in more detail at a human-centred curriculum, pedagogy and an approach to learning review. We offer guidelines regarding how to develop these areas within a human-centred school, including both principles and practical suggestions.

Note

1 Deep listening values the speaker, shows respect and appreciation and is caring. Such listening is healing, brings harmony into relationships and is the basis of all dialogue.

Chapter 3

A framework for a human-centred curriculum

Overview

In this chapter, we provide detailed guidelines concerning how to co-create a human-centred curriculum in a secondary school. We propose that a human-centred education should focus on encouraging young people to be in the driving seats of their learning and take responsibility for their personal development within a learning community. For this reason, we conceive the curriculum as a map that characterises the landscape of such learning. It provides contours but not details.

Briefly, we will first introduce the following seven key curriculum areas and then provide detailed advice and suggestions in terms of how to engage in each area through teaching and learning activities.

- Direction Time;
- Group Time;
- Cognitive Development Time;
- Individual Project Time;
- Specialist Subject Time;
- General Knowledge Time;
- Exploration Time.

One can think of educational planning as an interconnected triad consisting of curriculum, pedagogy and evaluation. Bernstein[1] (1977, 1990) calls these 'the pillars of education'. The main purpose of a curriculum is to specify the kinds of educational processes and activities that students ought to engage in. A curriculum provides a second-order general framework for first-order lesson plans. It is a map for making recipes.

What do the HCE principles say about how curricula should be constructed for young people in secondary schools?

First, it suggests that such a curriculum must treat students as human beings. Among other things, this means that it needs to provide spaces primarily for the young person's individual holistic development, and for meeting their current needs. For instance, the curriculum will provide time and space for developing relationships and expressing emotions, and for discussing issues concerning these. These spaces will also serve for collective reflection on what counts as development for each individual.

Second, a human-centred curriculum will provide opportunities for students to learn to be more caring towards other people.

Third, it will be tailored to the needs and talents of the individual and, therefore, it will be personalised. For example, if a student is hampered by a severe lack of self-confidence then there needs to be opportunities for the student to address this. Ideally, no one would be forced to take courses that have no meaning for them and for which they have no interest, and a person with a special talent in, say, mathematics would be able to take advanced classes. The curriculum needs to be appropriate or fitting for the individual. In this way, a human-centred curriculum should start from where a young person is, address their needs and overcome any blocks they have to self-development and learning.

Fourth, it will be based primarily on the development of human qualities or virtues rather than merely on the acquisition of knowledge and skills. This doesn't rule out knowledge and skill learning! Rather, it means that such learning can be part of a wider educational context rather than being treated as primary. Knowledge learning is a very important aspect of the personal development of the student, which will include the strengthening of academic virtues such as caring about details.

Traditional knowledge-based curricula are founded on the presupposition that a student needs a solid grounding in the knowledge of a subject area so that he or she could take advanced classes later on. This means that many students who won't follow the subject later are forced to learn material that has very little meaning for them. This time would be better spent enabling the student to appreciate the area of knowledge and to have a working understanding of basic principles.

A human-centred approach will nurture virtues that involve caring for things of value beyond oneself. The curriculum will be designed to include time for learning to care for areas of knowledge. It presents a challenge to the student's motivation. To be challenging in this way, the curriculum will offer a wide variety of activities and experiences so that the student has the opportunity to taste other areas of knowledge and to connect these to human life and work. These could include, for instance, explorations both outside the school and that go beyond the school curriculum.

Finally, a human-centred curriculum will enable the young persons to take responsibility for their own development and life path. Thus, it will encourage proactive self-guidance and hence, the internalisation of relevant standards.

In order for the young person to develop autonomy, there will need to be time for independent projects. Starting from the student's own interests and capacities, these processes will increasingly challenge the young person to reach out to new areas of knowledge and to new kinds of self-understanding and self-care. Such processes nurture the development of the student's initiative.

In general, a human-centred curriculum will offer not only spaces for guidance, challenge and direction, but also for self-reflection, peer interaction and exploration. In this way, it encourages an appreciation and understanding of external standards. For this reason, evaluation and feedback need to be part of this overall process of self-development so that teachers and others understand how best to support each student's learning.

The outline of seven key curriculum areas

Given the HCE principles and their application to curriculum construction, we will now present a suggestion for each of the seven mutually supportive curriculum areas, which together make up a human-centred curriculum. Each of these areas is connected to specific pedagogical practices for teachers, as we shall see in the next chapter.

Although this is not the only form a human-centred curriculum might take, we propose the following as a model that explicitly organises school time according to the aims of HCE. These aspects can easily be integrated into schools' specific contexts.

Recalling the HCE core curriculum triad introduced in Chapter 1, the time slot for guiding the student's holistic human development is the central hub of one's experience, which is supported by opportunities to develop emotionally and cognitively in very direct ways. The students also need time for project work, which is designed to cultivate their own initiative. In conjunction with this, the student also needs time to develop more specialised understanding and knowledge, as well as opportunities to gain relevant general knowledge and explore new areas of human knowledge and activity.

For these reasons, we have developed the seven curriculum areas as follows:

- *Direction Time:* This is led by a Mentor who will ideally work with the student for the entire duration of the three to four years of their secondary education. Mentoring sessions provide a space for the students to be guided in order to internalise educational standards, identify their talents, interests and preferred field of work in later life, review their progress in learning and be gently challenged towards self-awareness and self-guidance.
- *Group Time:* This includes both peer-led sessions, where small groups of students meet to discuss each person's progress, and more intense group sessions directed at emotional sharing and personal development and facilitated by a professional Facilitator. All sessions are open-ended in focus and integrate a variety of activities, such as dialogue, contemplation, drama, arts, music and movement, and other creative therapeutic approaches, allowing young people to explore their emotional landscape and discuss relationship issues in a safe, caring environment. We must bear in mind that emotional time is not aimed at sorting out emotional issues in order to perform well academically, or to motivate the students to focus on the academic work. Emotions are an important part of being human and we want young people to feel well and to flourish.
- *Cognitive Development Time:* This part of the curriculum is guided by the Cognitive Coach and is devoted to critical thinking, reasoning and self-conscious understanding of how one directs one's attention and uses one's cognitive abilities. It aims to cultivate the student's capacity to listen and speak, and read and write, as well as the more abstract thinking capabilities such as comprehension, systematic analysis, argumentation, deduction, criticism, questioning and making relevant connections. In other words, when students have the opportunity to develop and expand their intelligence, they are less likely to become disaffected by the external imposed curriculum.
- *Individual Project Time:* This is dedicated time for the students to develop their own project(s) directed by a Project Supervisor. The project might include vocational training, work experience, social work, academic work in the form of an inquiry, or a combination of the above. The aim is for the students to have learning experiences that relate directly to the kinds of activities they are interested in and might want to pursue later in life.

- *Specialist Subject Time:* This is taught by Academic Tutors and meets each student's need for knowledge, skills and virtues in a more specialised area. When a student has an increased self-awareness and a clearer direction in life, this part of the curriculum can serve two purposes. It can enable them to connect to subject contents, which points their attention outwards. Furthermore, it can help them to improve the relevant skills, attitudes and aptitudes, pointing attention inwards in a more self-reflective way. The latter is also being developed during Cognitive Development Time.
- *General Knowledge Time:* This part of the curriculum consists of brief and concentrated units that build into short, intense modules. These units are taught by Academic Tutors and are designed for students who are ready to learn and have sufficient background skills to understand and benefit from the general knowledge unit. General Knowledge Time can be integrated with Specialist Subject Time.
- *Exploration Time:* This part of the curriculum is organised and facilitated by the Mentors and provides opportunities for students to broaden their horizons. It involves engaging in a full range of activities within the school, including sports and physical activities, arts, drama and music activities, clubs, academic groups, school meetings and so forth. It also includes experiences outside of the school, for example taster sessions at higher education, visits to work places, services in the community, and so on.

These seven curriculum areas mutually support each other. For instance, in Direction Time, the students reflect on who they are and their learning experiences as a whole. In Group Time, they learn to understand their own emotions and those of others, and become confident both in who they are and in caring for others and for their learning. With such self-awareness, through exploration and studying general knowledge, the students further consolidate their interests and develop a sense of direction in life. This, in turn, motivates and guides their project work and enables a positive attitude towards cognitive and subject knowledge development.

In the rest of this chapter, we will expand on each of these curriculum areas.

Direction Time

In a human-centred school, each student is allocated a Mentor who oversees, supports and guides their educational journey. The Mentor works with the students on a one-on-one basis to co-construct their personalised learning experiences.

Direction Time mostly takes place at regular weekly meetings. When the student is progressing well, one weekly session will often be sufficient. During these weekly sessions, the Mentor provides feedback, direction, support and challenge to the student. Direction Time offers the opportunity for the student to frame their activities and life (both educational and otherwise) in more meaningful ways, and to embrace the challenges of an education.

Preparatory processes

1 *Building rapport and understanding.* An experienced Mentor will be able to take appropriate steps and deploy creative strategies to build rapport with each student. For some, a life history interview may be a helpful start during the initial mentoring

sessions. The life history interview provides a clear but also safe structure for students to talk about themselves and their lives so far, including their childhoods, significant people in their lives, earlier learning and educational experiences, dreams and hopes and also fears and inhibitions. Ideally, a Mentor offers his or her life history in return to help build the relationship. These initial conversations would take about two hours, and must take place in a private and quiet setting within the school.

2 *Preparing for the process.* The Mentor should introduce the young person to the idea of learning as holistic self-development. He or she should also explain clearly what the mentoring sessions are and how they support the student's personal development. This process will be gentle, caring and direct so that the young person does not feel forced and invaded. It is vital that the young person is, at the very least, a willing partner in the process.

Personal processes

Direction time should enable the student to go through deep personal processes in synergy with the other parts of the curriculum.

1 *Helping the student to care for him or herself.* Direction Time enables the students to become increasingly responsible for their development, and to feel the ownership of their learning processes. In part, it does this by posing questions such as, 'What am I doing in school, and why?' and by providing the students with opportunities for appreciative self-reflection. These exercises can lead the students towards thinking about their life as a whole – past, present and future.

    These processes will help the student develop the qualities related to a growing sense of self, such as self-respect, compassionate self-awareness, self-guidance and practical wisdom. These processes nurture the student's independence and sense of responsibility for their learning.

2 *Helping the student to engage.* Another key aspect of Direction Time is to enable and strengthen the young person's engagement with things beyond their own life, such as encouraging them to care about important social and global problems and areas of knowledge. This caring can be extended to the need to know relevant facts and understand key principles. During Direction Time, the student's capacity to question is stimulated and nurtured, leading to greater curiosity and care. All of these forms of caring can grow into engagements with the world around them, which can be nurtured during Direction Time. In other words, all knowledge learning starts with the felt need to know. All capacity building starts with the felt need to do.

3 *Helping the student to care for others.* The same points apply to the young person's caring for their friends and family. Relationships are a very important aspect of life and a holistic learning process will involve deepening and improving these relationships. Part of this is to appreciate better how other people see and feel things differently from oneself.

4 *Helping the student to understand the process.* In the above three areas, Direction Time helps the young person to connect with the values of their educational experiences and make sense of them as a whole. This has two steps. First, the young person needs to understand what counts as improvement in any area. With the guidance from the Mentor, further reflection on questions such as 'Given this, how can

I improve?' can provide the student an opportunity to internalise the standards for 'better' and 'worse' and thus, understand what would constitute improvement in education and how to improve. Second, Direction Time provides the young person with the opportunity to see the value and meaning of these improvements, and how these parts of their educational journey make sense within an overall picture of their life.

5   *Helping the student towards better self-understanding.* All of the above processes will help the student to an increased understanding of him or herself. Through these, students will be better able to identify what blocks them, what challenges they need to meet and what they need to work through. A student may co-construct a brief narrative concerning their strengths and weaknesses. Likewise, Direction Time can help enable the student to identify their talents, interests and preferred field of work in later life. In the end, this will lead towards an improved understanding of what would count as a good life for them as an adult, and what they need to do now to pursue such a life in the future.

Bringing these processes to fruition

More specifically, during Direction Time the Mentor helps the students to:

- identify challenges and obstacles, for example lack of confidence, inability to manage distractions, having difficulty in understanding academic standards, social emotional concerns, and so forth;
- nurture their capacities and develop strategies to overcome challenges and obstacles;
- identify important strengths and weaknesses;
- identify the personal qualities that they need to develop, for example patience, curiosity, questioning, and so forth;
- identify the skills to improve, such as reading, writing or critical thinking;
- identify the areas of knowledge that they need and want to learn;
- identify the activities they need to undertake over specific time periods, for example a week, month, term and year;
- set goals and prioritise them;
- construct a personal Learning Agreement (see below);
- design a personalised curriculum and timetable within the overall constraint of the school;
- review feedback from teaching staff and from peers.

Learning Agreement

Mentors might encourage their students to sign a Learning Agreement as it not only helps clearly outline the student's goals and priorities, but also allows the student to revisit their plans and contextualise their progress accordingly. A Learning Agreement also enables both student and Mentor to review progress over time. In other words, it can include a narrative that helps contextualise their goals. Therefore, a Learning Agreement would be adjustable and amendable as necessary, and would be applicable for a limited period, such as a semester.

The Mentor helps the student to identify three levels of trajectory and their associated goals:

1   *Immediate trajectories and goals*. These would include the full range of personal development goals based on the personalised curriculum of the student. They needn't be restricted to the seven elements of the curriculum, however. It is more important that the articulated goals touch the life of the student. These goals would have a short-term cycle such as a week or a month, and would tend to be specific.

2   *Intermediate trajectories and goals*. These would be goals for a whole term or academic year. Over such a period, the goals can be deeper, more personal and less specific, as well as include goals that are more academic.

3   *Overarching trajectories and goals*. These would include life trajectories such as the student's preferred area of work as well as a personal statement of what kind of life they want to pursue. Such overarching goals are harder to articulate clearly but can be refined over time. These relate back to the intermediate and immediate goals.

Any statement of these goals would form part of the student's Learning Agreement, or statement of intent. The Learning Agreement would indicate some of the goals above as priorities and explain why. These narratives can enable the student to revisit their plans, contextualise their progress and review their processes. Below is an example of how the Self-Managed Learning College in England has been using the Learning Agreement as a core element of its programme design.

Box 3.1 An illustration of using a Learning Agreement to encourage students' responsibility

The Self-Managed Learning College in England founded by Professor Ian Cunningham in Brighton, south-east of England, values learning with others and collaboration. There are three elements at its core: (1) learning agreement, (2) learning group, and (3) learning community. Self-managed learning combines structure and flexibility aimed at cultivating students' responsibility for their own and for supporting each other's learning.

The Learning Agreement comprises the student's answers to five questions which provide a robust framework for goal setting:

- Where have I been? (attending to past experiences relevant to a present goal).
- Where am I now? (examining current experience towards where to go next).
- Where do I want to get to? (setting personal goals).
- How will I get there? (imagining the journey of learning).
- How will I know I have arrived? (setting evaluative criteria).

Each learning group consists of six students and an adult learning group adviser who is specialised in facilitating learning and whose task is to ensure that the group meeting offers a unique space for each student. Students each have their own individual time and can discuss their learning experiences, report on progress and review how their activities contribute towards the goals identified in the Learning Agreement. Other members of the group listen, ask questions and challenge the student to go deeper in his/her learning.

As illustrated here, a Learning Agreement addresses the student's learning and developmental needs; the Mentor might also use the following five questions to guide the student:

1   How do I want to improve or develop during this term?
2   What do I want to learn in this term?
3   How will I develop and learn?
4   How will I document my development and learning?
5   How will I review my development and learning?

The first two questions help determine the student's broad learning objectives and priorities. The Mentor and the student will reflect together on more achievable goals but without losing sight of the necessary challenges the student might face based on their readiness.

The third question is to help the student to identify appropriate activities, for instance, lectures, classes, workshops, activities and so on, and necessary resources such as books and tools.

The fourth question is for the student to consider the ways they could record their learning process and express their learning, for example, as a written paper, a piece of artwork, and so on.

The last question is for them to reflect on what counts as good learning and how they might review progress.

The Learning Agreement can be used when the Mentor and the student review his or her overall progress over time. The student might also share Learning Agreement with a peer group who would provide further support, such as the way that the Self-Managed Learning College's case illustrates.

However, it is important to note that adolescents will need time to develop their vision for life, and identify their priorities. We wouldn't want them to make hasty and premature decisions about their plans. It is important to avoid the student feeling pressure to make decisions before he or she is ready and committing to a new whim every term or semester. Therefore, the Learning Agreement need not include everything! In any case, it is revisable, especially concerning the student's overarching trajectories and goals. It is also important that these aspects of the mentoring process do not become bureaucratic routines. In Chapter 4, we will outline how the Mentor can be attentive in this process.

Personalised curriculum

The significance of a Learning Agreement lies in its providing a framework for a student to follow a truly personalised curriculum.

The two overall qualities that the personalised curriculum needs to have are often in tension: on the one hand, the curriculum should be nurturing, and on the other, it should be challenging. As we have seen, Direction Time nurtures and challenges the student at the same time.

A fundamental aim of education is to cultivate the student's love of learning for its own sake. If a student is well-motivated to learn and develop, then for much of the learning process they may need only gentle guidance. If, on the other hand, a student is not motivated to learn then most of the school experiences will have little meaning for them. Therefore, Direction Time aims to connect the student to the appropriate motivation.

Ideally, this motivation points both outwards and inwards. Outwards it consists in connecting to areas of knowledge for their own sake. This means that the Mentor will pay special attention to the ways in which the students implicitly or subconsciously frame their learning processes. Pointing inwards, the motivation consists in the young persons feeling that they can have a bright and happy future, as well as having an understanding that their personal development will enable their future well-being and flourishing.

In Chapter 4, we will discuss more on this, especially in terms of how the Mentor uses Direction Time to nurture and challenge the student.

Reviewing and renewing the above processes

The process that we described in the 'Direction Time' above isn't necessarily linear and the cycle needs to be repeated on a regular basis. Quite apart from using feedback from other teachers to help articulate and modify goals, there needs to be a review of the student's overall development as part of the learning process. The review will allow the Mentor to discuss with students what they have done well and less well, and what they feel their greatest strengths and weaknesses are. Also using feedback from other staff, the Mentor will help the student arrive at a deeper and more holistic diagnosis, if possible.

Concluding comments

In general, Direction Time is the part of the curriculum in which students develop personalised learning plans and map out their overall learning needs so that their day-to-day schedules of activity converge in supporting their overall learning and growth trajectories.

The Mentor's professional qualities and pedagogical approach will be discussed in the next chapter of the handbook where we will outline some of the prerequisites for being a Mentor.

A well-trained Mentor needs to be creative in designing Direction Time. In Chapter 7, we will provide a list of training courses available for Mentors.

Group Time

Group Time is primarily dedicated to exploring, experiencing and understanding emotions and relationships. HCE in general concerns the development of the person as a whole. Given that emotions are a very important aspect of human life, the human-centred school will provide opportunities for emotional development as a priority. Likewise, our relationships with other people are a central and inescapable part of human life, both for adolescents and adults. Consequently, a human-centred curriculum will provide spaces for personal development concerning our emotions and our relationships with others.

The general aim of Group Time is to offer the opportunity to nurture some of the key emotional and relationship-related qualities that form part of the students' personal development. Such qualities concern caring about and for others, living and working in a group, and understanding one's own emotions, as well as those of others.

The first objective of Group Time is to enable young people to experience their emotions in direct ways that are perhaps not encouraged in other social settings in which individuals are implicitly asked to hide and even to deny their feelings. Group Emotional Time remedies this tendency.

The second objective is to provide the opportunities for young people to share their emotions with others of roughly similar age, in a non-judgemental, safe, confidential and small-group setting. Such sharing can be therapeutic and liberating. Also, it can encourage and nurture caring and an emphatic understanding of others.

The third objective is to provide a space for young people to reflect on their feelings and those of others. The process of experiencing and sharing emotions may be intense, and from this shared intensity there will follow the need to share in a more reflective manner on the nature and meaning of human emotions and relationships and how they fit into one's life.

The fourth and final objective is to provide young persons with the opportunity to explore ways in which their gained understandings regarding the above might apply to their present and future lives. These might include more creative and practically oriented workshops.

In some ways, the experiences of the first three of these four objectives can be grouped together. Thus, we suggest that Group Emotional Time consist of three kinds of sessions: (1) facilitated emotional time in a group, (2) peer mutual support time and (3) sessions pertaining to the creative and practical application of emotional and support time.

Group Emotional Time

The ideal size of an adult-facilitated group is no more than twelve young people. While the design of these sessions will vary greatly according to the Facilitator, it will have four main components, which are typically interwoven.

Four components of Group Emotional Time

a   The first and most important part is an *experiential* component. This might involve the use of group dynamics, role-play exercises, group team building and other similar activities to enable the young person to experience directly emotions, feelings and emotive perceptions. These sessions would take place in an informal setting that, if possible, is not a classroom. Through these sessions, the young people can feel, sympathise, empathise, laugh and cry together. In this manner, they learn to build caring attitudes. Sometimes people are blocked from their capacity to care for others and themselves by anger, fear, anxiety and sadness. These experiential activities would help young people to unblock these feelings and experience them directly.

> ### Box 3.2 An example of the experiential component of Group Emotional Time
>
> The group sit silently in a circle, anticipating. The door opens and a barefoot woman enters dressed in flowing silks, a veil shadowing her face. She is led to a chair in the centre of the circle, an empty chair is placed opposite. She lifts her veil, showing her closed eyes and placid countenance. The group sit, silent, hardly daring to breathe, unsure, an occasional glance at a friend, a timid peek at the

facilitator. The students are invited, in their own time and if they wish, to sit with the woman, and to look in her eyes . . . No one dares. The silence draws out. A giggle from one or two. Silence again. Liam, daunted by the strain, shifts loudly in his seat, leans back far, pushing his feet into the circle with a sigh. More silence. Stillness. Arthur looks around, stands and walks with an air of assurance and resignation to the centre and takes the chair.

The woman opens her eyes and looks into those of Arthur's, acknowledging each other with a tiny smile. The group watches, rapt, as the pair look at each other in silence, perfectly still. Twenty minutes pass. Arthur stands up and returns to his place in the circle. All is as before but now no one is shuffling. The woman's eyes are closed. Tahir launches himself from his seat and finds himself facing the woman. The emotions are clear on his face – defiance at first, then gratitude and finally love. Anita is next, who seldom speaks a word in group sessions. She sits, bathed in the warmth and acceptance of the woman's gaze but does not flinch. The group watch in awe as the woman in silk remains herself, whilst Anita's eyes welling up in tears.

(Extract from Eton-Slough-Hounslow ISSP Evaluation Report, 2016)

b   The second component is *sharing*. While the experiential component helps the young persons to experience emotions directly, the sharing part enables them to listen to the emotional experiences and feelings of others, as well as to communicate openly with others about their own. Sharing enhances and transforms the experience. It can be deeply touching to see others expressing their feelings. In this manner, the second component helps the young persons to develop their capacity to listen sympathetically, to understand others and to care more about how other people feel. After such experiences, a young person will be more able and willing to communicate with an open heart to others.

c   The third component is *encounter*. The encounter can be at many levels such as religion, culture, ethnicity, sexuality and gender. We envisage this as an intimate exchange in which young people may open up with regard to their self-perceptions and their concerns about others' perceptions of themselves. Equally, the encountering of diversity and differences provides the group with an opportunity to reflect on how individuals are identified and how relationships might be developed that simultaneously embrace and transcend differences.

d   The fourth is a *reflective* component. If the group goes through some deep or difficult or special experiences, then they may want to reflect collectively about what has happened and why. This component is different from the sharing one. In the sharing sessions, one imparts and communicates one's feelings, emotions and relationship experiences. In the reflective sessions, one tries to step out of those emotions, and so forth in order to reflect upon them.

Although it is up to the group what they want to discuss, the Facilitator ought not to relinquish responsibility to guide the topics and the discussions so that they contribute to the emotional development of the participants.

Furthermore, since the reflective discussions might become less intimate than the experiential, sharing and encounter activities, the Facilitator will be sensitive about the transitions towards this more impersonal psychological space. For instance, if the group is coming to an important climax or stage in an emotional or sharing process, then it shouldn't be interrupted by a discussion in which the young people express and interchange thoughts rather than feelings. If the participants are more likely to be speaking and listening from their heads than their hearts then it is better to keep the intimate and open space alive and introduce a more reflective discussion in a different context.

We suggest that there be at least two half-day sessions per term dedicated to the group sessions described above. As these often involve intense emotional experiences and sharing, it is more appropriate to have Group Emotional Time in the afternoon so that after these sessions the students can simply relax or reflect further, rather than return to other curriculum activities. Spending half a day with the group is likely to help participants feel more comfortable with one another and thus, make sharing experiences deeper and more fruitful.

Contextualisation

In all four components, the group sessions should be carefully contextualised in order that the young people can understand what these are about. Contextualisation also ensures that the created psychological space feels safe and welcoming for the individuals. This mutual sense of what this psychological space is for needs to be constructed with the involvement of the young people themselves so that it is less authoritarian.

It is thus pivotal that the young people shouldn't feel coerced or forced to participate. This is a space for them as individuals. They are not being made to do anything. At the same time, the group will agree to certain communication principles in order for the space to be safe. Such principles will include, for instance, the need to listen non-judgementally and compassionately to what people say, to respect confidentiality and privacy and to speak for oneself and from one's own feelings.

In addition, these sessions are not designed with a hidden academic agenda. They are not a means to help them perform better academically or in exams. They are for the young people to experience and to share as they want. This is time for their own development, and for this reason, the young people need to have a minimal sense of the idea of personal development. For instance, they will need to have the understanding that one's capacity to care for oneself and for others is impeded by feelings of anger, anxiety and sadness, and that when one can, it is better to confront and express these feelings rather than to let them simmer. Such concepts will become clearer during the processes themselves.

Group Facilitators

Typically, teachers are not trained how to facilitate such personal development workshops. However, most local communities do have people whose professions are to run such workshops, and who have experience in dealing with emotionally intense and potentially conflictive situations. Therefore, we recommend that the school seeks such skilled professional facilitators, despite budgetary constraints. However, it is important that the school articulates clearly the developmental purposes of these sessions to any facilitator. The school cannot delegate the formulation of its own aims for their students to the facilitators. Insofar as the school is trying to follow the HCE principles, it should keep to the ideas articulated within this handbook and the accompanying text. For more on the qualities of the Facilitator, see Chapter 4.

Consents

Another aspect for the school to consider is student and parental consent and responsibility. Parents need to understand that their children may go through psychological processes as part of their development. Likewise, of course, the young people themselves should appreciate the need for the processes. We imagine that the Group Emotional Time sessions can be emotionally powerful. Young people often live intensively in their own feelings. Therefore, there are issues concerning good practice as well as responsibility and liability. Schools might be worried about concerns such as 'What happens if a student becomes disturbed as a result of these sessions?' or 'What happens if a student becomes violent as a result?' The school needs to develop policies and procedures, as well as provide consent forms. A trained psychologist and counselor can offer alternative psychological work for young people with severe emotional difficulties. Likewise, a therapist or counselor should be available to give support to students who experience difficulties during these group sessions.

Mutual Support Time

The idea of Mutual Support Time is that students support each other in all aspects of their personal development and life at the school. This would not be restricted to the academic nor to the emotional and social relations. It could cover anything pertaining to mutual support.

These are best as peer-led group sessions (ideally five or six students per group). As such, they tend to be much more informal but they can offer an important opportunity for young people to work together and support each other. During peer-led group sessions, the young people learn to be there and care for each other. The safety of the small group and the closeness between the members mean that they can be both supportive and critical at the same time.

An adult Facilitator would help set up some guidelines for the peer-led sessions, such as respecting each person, valuing everyone's voice and input, listening empathetically, taking turns to speak, no gossiping, and so on.

The students take turns to be the 'chair' whose task it is to ensure that the conversation remains open, inclusive and genuine by guiding the group to keep to the guidelines. The student facilitator will also be responsible for making sure that the conversation is fruitful within the time limits. For example, if a pointless conversation threatens to use up all the time, then the student facilitator would be responsible for moving the conversation along.

Otherwise, these sessions are intended to be open-ended. Young people choose their own topics during peer-led sessions, including reviewing and supporting each other's goals and priorities set out in their respective Learning Agreements. The topics should be relevant to the individuals' current concerns, such as friendship issues, struggles with homework and relationship challenges at home or at school.

An adult Facilitator needs to be on hand for these sessions. All students should take part in ongoing training in peer facilitation. It is an opportunity for young people to develop leadership capacities and caring attitudes. It is a good idea for the young person who is facilitating a session to speak with the adult Facilitator both before and after the session. In this way, the young person can receive some tips and encouragement, and can debrief after the experience.

There could be up to two peer-led group sessions of thirty minutes each week.

Other Group Time sessions

A larger group of twelve to fifteen young people might have opportunities for learning experiences together that are less directly emotional but which, nevertheless, are important for life.

We suggest that the school curriculum includes time slots for three types of session:

1   The first is a *creative* session using artistic outlets such as visual arts, music, poetry and drama. Such activities encourage young people who are less verbal about feelings and personal relationships to find alternative and non-threatening ways to express themselves.

2   The second is *group discussion* centred on themes and topics related to the affective and social aspects of one's life. Possible topics include questions pertaining to relationships with one's peers, friendship and intimacy, peaceful communication, the limits of responsibility, how to deal with one's own feelings and how to go about problem-solving with sensitivity and care. The adult Facilitator will guide the young people in the selection of topics and themes.

3   The third is a *practical* session. It offers the opportunity for young people to explore topics related to the practical side of adult life such as money management, workload management, household management, parenting and being part of a family and other homemaking topics. Some of these could be conducted as group discussions, but others could be brief presentations perhaps from outside speakers, including the parents of current students.

Box 3.3 An example of group discussion

It is near the end of the first session and the group seems tired, fidgety and ready to go home. The short video starts, an evocative depiction of the discrepancies between how others see us, and our own self-image, and immediately the whole group sit captivated.

As the video ends, students glance at each other nervously, not entirely sure how to cope with the emotionally charged atmosphere in the room. When invited to share their feelings, Carla confesses she wants to cry. Several others nod. Ali recounts the message of the video at length, speaking with enthusiasm. Although not directly expressing how he feels, Ali's body language suggests that he feels energised, engaged and inspired.

The young people and the adult Facilitators then share together many personal anecdotes, acknowledging and revealing their own vulnerabilities around self-image and the insecurity they sometimes experience. Richard says:

Everyone seemed to open up as it seemed to be a mutual feeling (insecurity) and one that everyone could relate to. This was my most enjoyable session and really got me interested in the rest of the project.
(Extract from Eton-Slough-Hounslow ISSP Evaluation Report, 2016)

The example in Box 3.3 shows that such group sessions can have a profound impact on students' experiences of emotions, which in turn impact their well-being. We would suggest at least one thirty-minute session each week for this purposes.

Concluding comments

For a young person to develop holistically, they need time for their feelings to grow and opportunities to learn from this in a very personal way, albeit with others.

In this section, we have suggested how different curriculum components might support such emotional processes. In addition, we recommend that the school establish fora for feedback from the Facilitators to the Mentors. As we have seen, the main role of the Mentor is to bring together all the learning processes of the young person into a significant and purposeful whole that changes according to the student's needs. This must include the Group Time. Therefore, the Facilitators in charge of Group Time ought to work closely with the Mentors.

Cognitive Development Time

Cognitive Development Time is a time when young people can develop sensitivity to language and learn to navigate all kinds of texts with a critical eye.[2] These skills will enable them to develop qualities and capabilities to participate in subject studies and project work, as well as support them to make critical judgements about the world around them and guide them in making good decisions throughout life.

Cognitive Development Time involves focused coaching sessions individually or in small groups with a Cognitive Coach. Cognitive Development Time addresses the cognitive developmental needs of each student from their present condition, based on a simple evaluation. The Cognitive Coach liaises with the student's Mentor and Academic Tutors in order to help construct an individualised cognitive coaching programme for the student based on the evaluation and conversations with the student. Therefore, this part of the curriculum will be responsive and understanding of the student's needs.

We strongly recommend creating a distinct time period for cognitive development. It is an opportunity for the student to develop their cognitive capacities and skills explicitly and directly, without the pressures of trying to understand some subject matter.

This has two important advantages. First, it encourages the student to think self-consciously and explicitly about their cognitive development, while at the same time providing space to act on this self-understanding. This may enable issues related to anxiety and self-confidence to emerge and to be addressed explicitly. The increased self-understanding will support the student in becoming more self-responsible, a process that is integral to their work with the Mentor.

Second, if used well, time spent in this way will reap good rewards in other areas. It will enable the student to make faster progress in many other aspects of their study. The failure of many students to engage fully with what happens in a classroom may be understood to stem in part from weaknesses in their cognitive capacities. In particular, students may suffer from a lack of necessary competences with regard to language and may have never properly developed their abilities to read, which we consider a fundamental skill.

Cognitive skills come in stages and there is little point in teaching a student the capacities associated with a later stage, such as writing, if they do not have basic skills in both reading and listening and some appreciation of their importance.

Overall, Cognitive Development Time has four key components: (1) reading, (2) listening, (3) thinking, and (4) speaking and writing. Let's examine each of these in detail.

Reading

We have identified four levels in developing the art of reading, which form part of the student's cognitive growth. These do not exclude the idea that there are other important practices and stages. To a large degree, it depends on the kind of text in question. In this section, we will not discuss literature such as novels and poems.

At the elementary level, *reading aloud*. Many young people may read very fast and have not learned how to find emphasis and intonation in their reading. In brief, they have not been taught how to read a book as if the text were speaking to them. A reader needs to know how to make a book come alive. Therefore, it is important to practise the art of reading aloud until it transforms the way in which one reads silently.

At the next level, students need to learn how to *get an overview* of what they read. For example, they may need to know how to extract the main point from a piece of discursive prose and how to map the structural features of a chapter or section around this main point or conclusion. When a student learns to do this, they will be able to signal which parts of a text are vital or crucial to understand and thereby, be able to discern when to spend more time on comprehending a passage and when not to do so.

There is an important aspect to the art of gaining an overview of a text. Most people read only for the content and in effect ask themselves the question 'What is the author or the text saying?' This is one way to discern the topology of a text: the landscape changes when the subject matter or topic changes. However, it is also necessary to answer the question 'What is the author doing now?' For example, an author could be making their main point, explaining or qualifying the main point, answering an objection, clearing up a misunderstanding, showing the implications of the main point or explaining why they are important. If one answers the question 'What is the author doing now?' then one can find the major transitions in the text, and thereby more easily obtain an overview.

One way to see these transitions in a text is to look at the headings of the sections within a chapter. If there are no headings or if one needs to discern the transitions within a section, then one can do so by reading the first sentence of each paragraph and noting the transitions or changes in what the author is doing.

At this level of development, practising *note taking* and *text mapping* becomes a key to strengthening reading. Young people are ready to *take notes* of what they read. Usually, students aren't taught to take good notes. Nevertheless, it is an art well worth acquiring, which will improve the student's overall quality of reading. Most students need to learn how to take concise notes with which they can acquire an overview of the text and select what is important.

In order to be able to take good and concise notes on a text, it is necessary to be able to map the contours of the text and identify the main points or conclusions. In other words, a student should be able to say something like, 'There are five important points in the chapter'. Often, chapters consist of four or five main points; the text prior to a main conclusion explains it, and the text afterwards outlines its importance or implications.

At a later level, the young person may need to learn how to identify the argumentation or reasoning in a piece of prose. To do so means that they are able to identify the conclusion of the piece of reasoning and are able to articulate the steps that the author goes through to arrive at that conclusion.

Later still, the student needs to be able to criticise a piece of prose writing. This requires, however, that they are able to separate clearly what the text means from their own thoughts about it. This involves being willing and able to not be too quick in their critique. It also means that they have a robust sense of what a relevant criticism is. It further requires that they are able to distinguish critiques of the position from criticisms of the argument or evidence for the position: a badly supported claim isn't necessarily a false assertion.

Listening

Of all the basic cognitive skills, listening is possibly the most neglected. Most of the cognitive capacities mentioned above that need developing with regard to reading are much harder to exercise with respect to listening. For example, it is harder to hear the structure of a lecture or speech than it is to see the organisation of a written chapter. Therefore, these capacities need to be developed first with respect to written texts.[3] Once the student has a basic intuitive grasp of these skills in relation to a piece of writing, they can apply them to a speech or discourse. This ability might best be nurtured by taking notes of complex lectures or presentations.

One of the ways in which listening is more challenging than reading is that a person is more predisposed to non-consciously impose their personal interpretations on content that is spoken than on something written. In part, this is because the latter invites a more considered interpretation. In other words, prejudices are more active in listening than in reading. This means that we can help students listen with less bias and with a more open mind by asking them to transfer their reading abilities to the art of listening.

This is why taking notes of a lecture or a conversation is a more challenging exercise than doing the same for a piece of reading. The same applies to the mapping of a lecture or speech. We can use this point to help the student. Once the young person has some skill in taking notes from a written piece, we can challenge them to do the same with a lecture and then afterwards with a discussion. All of these exercises would have the aim of helping students to attend to and identify the conclusions and structure of what is said.

Thinking and reasoning

As already mentioned, the growth of cognitive capacities comes in stages, and the development of the basic skills and cultivation of appreciation of their importance can serve as the preliminary steps to approaching later stages of cognition, such as critical reasoning and applied logic that emphasise informal fallacies. It may not make sense to teach a student these informal fallacies if they don't have in place at least two prerequisites.

First, it has to make sense motivationally. The student must have a sense that their life would be transformed for the better if they were able to activate their intelligence, and that this requires the learning of certain skills. Often students have an apathy concerning their intelligence because of, for instance, misplaced low self-esteem. This means that Cognitive Development Time sessions need to be respectful and caring in this regard. In the context of such a safe space, students may be able to appreciate the importance of their own cognitive capacities.

Second, students need to have more than a minimal sensibility to words. Some students have a limited vocabulary and do not have much sensitivity to the meanings of words. Such students need exercises that increase both their vocabulary and their sensitivity to word meaning. For instance, some people are less aware of the differences between the meanings of words that may seem to be close neighbours. Again, apathetic students may not have a sense of why these semantic skills are an important aspect of their development. Therefore, we suggest that students are given exercises on the meaning of words and the differences between words that are similar. Some of our favourites are: 'well-being' and 'happiness'; 'desire' and 'need'; 'loving' and 'falling in love'.

These are prerequisites to the teaching of the techniques and rules of informal logic. HCE teaches us that any course on critical reasoning needs to have an emotional relevance and a cognitive foundation in the state of the student before it can have educational significance.

Thinking and reasoning skills are to some extent cultivated in the way students learn about reading. These are connected to helping students understand the nature of argument, distinguish different types of arguments, develop skills to set up arguments with logic and learn to analyse and evaluate arguments, and to identify fallacies.

When the students are motivated to think logically and critically using the linguistic sensitivity they developed in the earlier stages, Cognitive Development Time will further cultivate their confidence to think and reason clearly, to convince others of their points of view supported by plausible reasons and cogent arguments.

When students are motivated and engaged they are more likely to ask questions. So part of the cognitive coaching session is not only to encourage young people to ask questions, but also to foster curiosity in them and guide them to ask good questions. In this way, the students will learn to clarify meaning, as well as to make distinctions that affect their thinking and judgements, and clarify emotions, motives and desires that might influence their thinking.

Critical thinking and reasoning are perhaps best taught in the light of topics that are relevant to the students such as contemporary ethical issues, moral dilemmas, public policy debates and other topics within the media. By developing thinking skills, the young person also learns to care more for things that matter in the world. Once the student has reached a solid level of reasoning and care, critical thinking can be extended to more abstract and remote matters.

Speaking and writing

The final component of the cognitive skills component involves the capacities of speaking and writing. Since these capacities are interlinked, it would be wise to work on them together. Of course, there are differences between them and it will probably be easier to help a student with the more general aspects of their capacities when focusing on writing. For example, the following questions can be helpful for the student to consider when considering the qualities necessary in order to write well:

- What is the general point that you wish to make, or the main question that you wish to answer in this piece of writing?
- In the planning of your work, how would you best structure the text to make your point(s)?
- How would you avoid distractions (i.e. your own thoughts that distract you)?
- How do you articulate your ideas clearly?
- How do you edit after you have written the first draft?

In contrast, there are more specific capacities that are probably best addressed in relation to speaking. For example, if a young person consistently produces ungrammatical sentences and tends to use words in a way that are semantically inappropriate then the student may need to work on this with respect to their verbal communication first.

Most people have an implicit and intuitive sense of what counts as a better or worse use of language. They can feel when a spoken sentence isn't clear. This intuitive sense can be nurtured so that the person produces clearer sentences more often. In this regard, a student might agree to record a brief impromptu talk they give and then to critically assess it, with the guidance of the Cognitive Coach.

Integrating Cognitive Time within the curriculum

In general, a human-centred curriculum will encourage a student to reflect self-consciously and conceive what they are trying to attain in their education in new ways. Some of these perceptions will involve connecting better to values beyond him or herself. For example, when a student cares about what is true and false with regard to an area of knowledge, then he or she has connected to something valuable. The parts of the curriculum pertaining to, for instance, project work, specialist knowledge and exploration ought to reinforce such connections and caring. In contrast, some aspects of educational development concern self-development more exclusively. In this respect, Cognitive Development Time should be considered as an opportunity for self-investment. It is a time when the student can focus his or her attention on him or herself. It is an explicit opportunity for self-development. The Mentor and the Cognitive Coach need to enable the student to appreciate the value of cognitive development in its own terms: it is an opportunity to make one's intelligence more alive, active and strong.

Although we recommend a four-point outline of a programme, a school may wish to import new and different exercises into their Cognitive Development Time.

Box 3.4 An example of a cognitive development checklist

Korowal School in Australia regards students' cognitive development an important part of their problem-solving capacity and social communication development. Students are encouraged to apply sound independent judgement and to be intellectually proactive and persistent, and at the same time, to be creative, explorative and cooperative in their thinking.

The list of cognitive qualities and skills that Korowal School aims to develop (based on the recommendations of Cam, 2006) include:

- an enquiring outlook coupled with an ability to articulate problems and issues;
- a tendency to be intellectually proactive and persistent;
- a capacity for imaginative and adventurous thinking;
- a habit of exploring alternative possibilities;
- an ability to critically examine issues and ideas;
- a capacity for sound independent judgement.

Social habits that will be developed as a result of the above include:

- a habit of actively listening and of understanding others' points of view;
- a disposition to give reasons for what you say and to expect the same of others;
- a habit of exploring disagreements reasonably;
- a disposition to be generally cooperative and constructive;
- a disposition to be socially communicative and inclusive;
- a habit of taking other people's feelings and concerns into account.

The development of cognitive capabilities greatly affects the student's ability to learn the concepts and organising principles of different areas of knowledge, such as humanities, social studies, mathematics and the natural sciences. Much of this concerns how the student directs his or her attention. From this foundation, more abstract thinking capabilities can develop, including comprehension, systematic analysis, argumentation, deduction, criticism, questioning, making the relevant connections and choosing relevant strategies.

Indeed, if the Cognitive Development Time is appropriately introduced into the curriculum, an adolescent will develop progressively the capacity to reason abstractly, hypothetically and multidimensionally, to challenge the views of authors, to question accepted knowledge and to embrace uncertainty. They will also learn to become more systematic in solving problems, more logical in their deductions, and more capable of finding relevant facts and discarding the irrelevant. All these capacities are not only fundamental building blocks for their independence in academic studies; they are also key attributes for their work experiences later in adulthood and vital qualities for an enriched human life in general.

Furthermore, Cognitive Development Time is very important for the student's evaluative self-perception. Once a student has the basic capacities in reading, listening, thinking, speaking and writing, they will have the self-confidence to take these capacities to a new level. At this point, education can be deeply transformative. This is because, when a certain level of capacity and confidence is attained with respect to basic cognitive skills, the student can more easily draw nutrition from larger subject-based classes. In other words, the integrated personalised processes of mentoring, emotional sharing and cognitive training will help the student to attain a level such that more general class sessions become directly relevant to their personal development.

In other words, without a personalised educational process, we might reasonably expect the curriculum dedicated to knowledge and information to have little motivational relevance to many students. They wouldn't care so much about specialist and general knowledge. In contrast, with an appropriately personalised programme such as the triad (individual mentoring–Group Time–cognitive development) described so far, students begin to have a sense of their own self-worth and with this a better sense of their own development.

All conventional class teaching relies on students having sound cognitive abilities. A student may start out very interested in the subject matter, but if they do not have the skills to participate fully they will quickly lose their enthusiasm. Cognitive Development Time enables students to learn these skills in a focused, directed way, which in turn allows them to engage better with their other learning activities.

Cognitive Development Time is important to the life of young people outside the school. For instance, we expect that the development of a young person's cognitive capabilities will enhance their ethical sensitivity towards the perspective of others. They will become more aware of how others perceive and think, and hand in hand with this, they will become increasingly aware of their own biases and prejudices. As part of their cognitive development, the young person will learn to identify his or her ethical commitments and by thinking them through, this will foster clearer moral judgement. Strong thinking skills can be a foundation that runs through young people's lives in several ways. For instance, such skills will help them avoid needless quarrels, appreciate the viewpoint of others, clarify their own goals and help them to make better choices as members of a community.

In these ways, Cognitive Development Time mutually supports Group Emotional Time. Group Time enables young people to experience the raw feelings of others and Cognitive helps to bring this appreciation into their thinking processes. For this reason, it is important for the Cognitive Coach and the Facilitator to liaise with each other through the Mentor. For example, if a student has a breakthrough in Group Time, this may be an important opportunity for him or her to advance in Cognitive Development Time, for example, by becoming more aware about how to reason in ways that take into account the perspectives of others. Additionally, other components of a human-centred curriculum offer opportunities for students to develop these ethical and social qualities, as we shall see.

It is important to stress that Cognitive Development Time, like any other component of the curriculum, is concerned with qualities or virtues. In learning to read, listen, think and write better, the student will be developing appropriate ways of caring. This caring is not restricted to the ethical and social. For example, she will care about what a text means or about what the main conclusion of a section or chapter is. She will care more about whether the conclusion is true and what follows from it. The student will learn when it is important to pay careful attention to detail and when it is more important to attend to broad strategic points.

Cognitive Coaches will be experts in cognitive training, linguistic capability coaching and general philosophical training. They are skilled in facilitating small-group discussions, debates and collaborative thinking, as well as working with the student at an individual level. We will elaborate on the work of the Cognitive Coaches in the next chapter.

Given the importance of Cognitive Development Time, a minimum allocation of two or three sessions each week is necessary to help students develop such capabilities. The class size can vary, but it is much better if students work in small groups and even on an individual basis.

Individual Project Time

In Project Time, each student develops and works on their own project, under the guidance of both their Mentor and Project Supervisor. Project Time should provide a space for self-initiated processes of delving into something deeply.

Individual Project Time is an important ingredient in the curriculum because it allows for more ownership of, and proactive engagement with, the learning process and helps inculcate in the student a caring attitude for the quality of their work. If the student does become deeply engaged, then the project might form the basis of transformation and of greater involvement in other areas of learning.

Projects may include some combination of experience and study related to the kinds of activities the young person is interested in and might want to pursue later in life.

An independent project should embody three important qualities:

- The student needs to *feel ownership* of the project. This means that they would care about the project both in terms of the quality of their work and in terms of the subject matter involved in the project.
- The project needs to *be challenging for the student* in appropriate ways, and especially it will pertain to the development of their capacity for personal initiative. The project provides an opportunity for the student to exercise their initiative in relation to something that they care about, academic or otherwise. At the same time, the design of the project should challenge them to grow appropriately in other ways, such as their talents, horizons and self-perceptions. This is why the Mentor's input is valuable. The Mentor will have an overview of the student's needs and interests. Therefore, if the student is interested in art and is weak in mathematics, then a project that might interest but at the same time challenge

their abilities and horizons might be to make a business proposal for a new art gallery in the town centre.

- The project needs to *fit well with* the interests, talents and development trajectory of the student both in the present moment and in the near future. Thus, although it challenges them in various ways and requires initiative, the student needs to feel that they are in an area of life that fits a possible trajectory and their current interests. In short, it needs to be personally meaningful for the student, though not necessarily always in ways that they will immediately recognise.

A project might take several different forms. It might be based on work experience or social projects outside of the school; it could focus on academic work or an empirical research; it might be an exploration of business ideas, or the study of some vocation. Thus, a project may seek to answer a definite question, reflect on a particular social phenomenon or take the form of a report, a portfolio of art, a business plan, a design project or a paper. Students are encouraged to link their projects to experiences beyond academic study, and to develop a sense of self-responsibility and of self-guided learning. As we said before, while the student needs to feel ownership of the project, it has to challenge them and provide a space for the exercise of initiative.

For a project to take shape, the student would propose an initial idea with the guidance of the Mentor in Direction Time. The Mentor may need input from other staff members in order to guide the student towards a more meaningful and challenging project. Based on this input, the Mentor will encourage the student to pursue projects that relate meaningfully to their planned life projection, future work or course of study.

Once an initial and simple proposal is articulated in Direction Time, the Mentor will arrange for a student to meet with an appropriate member of staff who will act as their Project Supervisor. Depending on both the nature of the project and on the student's confidence and needs, the supervision may be more or less frequent or involved. The extent of involvement will be agreed between the student and the Supervisor and in some cases, the Mentor may also contribute their perspective on the level of support needed.

We suggest that the life cycle of Project Time should be at least one term (twelve weeks) and can be as long as the entire academic year. It is important not to rush the process of identifying the content and direction of the project. In some cases, the student can be working on research and writing even while the project plan is still under construction. It is equally important that the student has time to reflect on the process at the end. Therefore, completed projects could be due two to three weeks before the end of the school year so that there is time for debriefing and reflection.

For some students, the project cycle may consist in two or more parts. For example, by the start of September, a student might feel committed to research and write about a particular social problem. However, they may not have enough knowledge or understanding of the field to construct the plan of a complete project. Therefore, the first phase of the project might contain part of the research necessary to define the second and final phase of the work.

Due to the flexible nature of projects, there can only be general guidelines for project work. For instance, all project proposals might include the following:

1   a clear focus or answer a specific question;
2   a plan of action broken into steps, and an indicative timetable;
3   an articulation of the form of the completed project, for example a written report on a research inquiry; a specific production such as a fashion show, a concert or a fundraising event; or an artefact such as a piece of art, or a design;
4   a clear articulation of good standards (whatever constitutes the criteria for 'good' for this project);
5   an accompanying logbook documenting significant steps in the learning journey, including reflections on the process of the project.

We suggest that all students be expected to keep a project logbook to document their progress and experiences of significant learning. This helps to encourage self-reflective learning on the process itself. This would enable the student to think about what they need to develop as a person in terms of their cognitive capacities and personal qualities. These personal learning opportunities provide a space for exercising self-responsibility. Young people can learn to become their own 'gurus', eventually.

The example below shows that project work can make learning truly empowering and inspiring, and the Project Supervisors' main tasks have been to focus on nurturing the student's initiative throughout the process of project work by providing appropriate challenges, guidance with regard to the overall project processes, constructive feedback and caring support pertaining to the student's aims, approach and progress.

Box 3.5 Facilitating and supervising project work

At the Bina Cita Utama School in Indonesia, students heard speakers from the United Nations Industrial Development Organization talk about the health impacts of mercury brought about by illegal mining, not only on the miners themselves but also on others through water pollution. Some of the older students were curious about it and went into the field to see first-hand the devastating environmental effects of illegal mining, and they decided to embark on a project on the topic.

After the initial exploration, the students went ahead and formulated their own research questions and they worked in groups of three to pursue the inquiry. Each group focused on its own questions and decided on the methods by which to share the fruit of their inquiry. Some wrote detailed reports on their research findings, others put together posters to present the detrimental effect of illegal mining and others used art and cartoons to produce educational material aimed at awareness building.

Once they completed the projects, the teachers opened up a space for students to discuss how they would like to proceed to the next step. After long discussions, the young people decided to visit a local high school in an illegal mining area and present their projects to the children from the families of illegal miners about the health effects of mercury, and how simple devices can be used to trap and recycle the mercury.

The learning process was entirely driven by the students themselves, and the teachers were there to ensure that the space for exploration was open and that they had all the support they needed in order to meet the challenges they encountered. Through this facilitated process, students were able to make connections between their activities within the school and real-life problems.

Individual Project Time is self-directed learning time and therefore the allocation for it on the student timetable must be distinguished from general activity time. This is a designated learning time, either at the school or outside of it.

Specialist Subject Time

Specialist Subject Time provides training in traditional subjects that are compulsory as part of the student's education, or in subjects that the student would like to specialise. The areas of specialism need not be very specific; they depend on the individual and the context, but usually they would include subjects broadly within the natural sciences, social studies and humanities. This part of the curriculum offers courses so that the student can acquire knowledge and understanding that is important for their specialisations.

The national curriculum outlines the content of each subject area in a very systematic manner. These curricula have been developed over many years, and they are very helpful in ensuring that students have mastered essential subject knowledge and have acquired basic skills.

However, unfortunately such curricula tend to leave other areas of the student's learning and development relatively untouched. Therefore, a school that wants to be human-centred can try to re-orientate or reframe the traditional curriculum in various ways, without diminishing its quality.

First, it is important that the students connect to the valuable nature of what they are studying. For instance, stars are very interesting but to understand the life cycle of stars well, it is necessary to master some challenging mathematics, which requires some effort. Although we cannot expect young people to find *all* areas of knowledge captivating, nevertheless, we can hope that they will appreciate that all areas of study are intrinsically valuable, despite the challenges in connecting to them. We can also hope that each young person falls in love with some areas of knowledge about which they want to know more. The student's Mentor would be sensitive to such interests of the student, but the Subject Tutor might have insights worth sharing.

Second, it is vital that the students see the study of each subject as important and relevant for their own growth and development as a person. The time with the Mentor, and perhaps Group Time, will help in this respect. This means that the students will grasp how the qualities or virtues that form part of the discipline or subject can contribute positively to, or be part of, their own growth. Each discipline is constituted in part by a set of virtues that can be an integral part of a person's development. Therefore, a human-centred curriculum articulates these usually implicit disciplinary virtues as part of a student's self-development.

Whilst the Mentor has a primary responsibility in guiding this process, Tutors of the specialist subjects may need to join in this nurturing process. For example, they can explain why their subject is deeply interesting and they can seek out students who seem to be less motivated to find out why. In this sense, the importance of Subject Time isn't just the knowledge and skills that the students develop. It is also the feeling that things matter beyond the confines of their own lives. This feeling of care is a virtue.

Third, ideally, the students would treat Subject Time as an excellent opportunity to put into practice the capacities and aptitudes that they are developing in Cognitive Development Time. Hopefully, they can see these connections in practical terms as helping them to study and understand better. This is a vast area of synergy that the school can develop for the sake of its students.

Fourth, it is important that the students expand and deepen their interest in specific subject areas (except when they study them purely on the basis of their being compulsory). Therefore, it is the responsibility of the Mentor to ask the student to articulate what he or she finds interesting about such an area and why. It would also be useful to know why the student finds other related areas less interesting. As the Mentor helps the student to better understand these interests, they can work together to plant more 'seeds' of interest in the process of constructing the personalised curriculum. Personal choice is a key point of growth in this case.

General Knowledge Time

General Knowledge Time consists in brief and concentrated sessions built into modules that can serve as an overview of subjects and topics that a student might later want to pursue more intensely, for example, an overview of British History, an introduction to psychology or an introduction to religion. The idea of these introductory classes is to give the student a broad overview and general idea of a subject area. Thus, in the case of a history general knowledge session, the aim is not to make a historian out of a student, but rather to give them a general idea of history as a subject, an idea of particular aspects or periods of history, and an understanding of how the past has led to the present.

General Knowledge Time consists in short classes of thirty minutes for intensive learning. Keeping these sessions short can engage the students better. They are set in modules so that students who have been to basic-level classes can opt to attend more advanced classes on the same topic.

The Mentor is best suited to help the student choose appropriate modules and to oversee this process. The importance of this time for the young person is twofold.

On the one hand, the idea is to provide students with an opportunity to explore areas of knowledge without being committed to specialising in them. The idea is to stimulate and encourage their curiosity. The eventual aim is to enable the young persons to feel that they can connect meaningfully to areas of interest that lie beyond their speciality. In particular, we envisage that the general knowledge sessions will help the students to ask questions about things beyond their everyday life. In other words, it is part of the process of pointing the mind outwards towards the wider world.

On the other hand, general knowledge sessions form part of the process that can enable the students to integrate these learning experiences and knowledge into their own growth and become responsible for the process. In other words, it is part of the process of directing the attention inwards, towards oneself and one's own development.

Thus, the main task for teachers of General Knowledge Time is to disclose the interesting aspects of these knowledge areas without trying to sell them to the student. They offer the students the opportunity to connect the subject of study with other areas of knowledge, and thus, broadly to their own growth.

These characterisations of the meanings of General Knowledge Time point to the important responsibility of the Mentor during Direction Time. The Mentor will guide the student towards gaining general knowledge that they might find interesting without the students feeling coerced into a boring 'spectator sport'. Indeed, the Tutor also works closely with the students to ensure that the content of the Exploration Time sessions helps them in all of these directions of growth, through other curriculum areas such as Group Time, Cognitive Development Time and Independent Project Time.

Exploration Time

Exploration Time provides the opportunity for the students to broaden their horizons and explore new areas of knowledge that they might find interesting. This component in the curriculum aims to challenge their capacity to connect meaningfully to things beyond themselves and to open their minds to new possibilities. It also forms an important part of their self-understanding.

Broadly, Exploration Time involves four kinds of activities:

1   *Existing activities in the school.* Any student should be able to attend a class session or activity group that is new to them, under the guidance of their Mentor. This may mean that the student is an observer in some classes and an active participant in others. For example, a student who specialises in the natural sciences might want to explore themes in the humanities to see what they are missing.

2   *Special organised activities.* Both students and staff may propose activities that explore ideas beyond the normal curriculum. These are offered as a taster. These activities might be related to potential areas of work for students, for example, a participatory seminar that explains what lawyers do and explores the question 'Why is the law important to us?', a presentation related to healthcare, or a lecture on environmental protection. Such tasters help students get a sense of the world and work and this can form part of the slow process that enables them to identify activities of interest.

3   *Activities that occur outside of the school.* If a student has special questions or interests that aren't satisfied by knowledge studies but which are not yet formalised as a project, then they will need to devote time to the exploration of these topics. The point of Exploration Time is that the students are free of external pressures, such as arriving at a project proposal, because they are exploring for its own sake.

4   *Activities that the student does independently with little direction.* These could be reading a book, watching a documentary film or writing a novel. Students can propose activities for themselves or for a group as part of their exploration. They

are encouraged to take the initiative, liaise with staff and external parties and take overall responsibility for it.

During Exploration Time, the students focus on the experiences and the encounters. Although requiring little direction, it does mean that the Mentor offers a great deal of care, such as inviting the students to share experiences during their weekly conversations and encouraging them to draw insights from these encounters. Young people can be idealistic, but where there is a lack of nurturing, idealism may turn to cynicism. Through Exploration Time, the student would also be encouraged to reflect on questions such as, 'How can I contribute best to our society and to the world?' or, 'How can society be better organised?' The encounters of Exploration Time may prompt such reflection.

Box 3.6 Exploration Time at Bishop Park College

Here are two ways that Bishop Park College encouraged students to explore their interests and expand their horizons.

Fridays were given over to masterclasses. A class of students worked for the whole day with a teacher and focused on a particular topic, such as building and racing a model car, exploring a piece of literature through drama or creating a foreign language text to submit to a French website through language acquisition games and adaptation skills.

Faculty Days ran for three days at the end of term when the College would be divided across year groups and mini-schools, allowing students to work with both teachers and students they did not usually meet in their normal school day. Faculty projects were planned anew each year and provided a wonderful opportunity for students and staff to be at their most creative and imaginative. Often involving visits away from the College, topics ranged from researching and presenting Clacton-on-Sea in its resort heyday to researching the Norman Conquest and understanding why the Normans won, from creating a performance of Animal Farm from scratch to examining a member of staff's car for traces of forensic evidence and analysing it.

Exploration Time is not restricted to standard academic subjects. Since it aims to stimulate real (as opposed to idle) curiosity, it must involve topics that transcend traditional subjects. Thus, in part, the content can be built around the actual questions that students feel to be important. However, this point is subject to three important qualifications, which also apply to General Knowledge Time:

a   As young people are not always good at articulating their own interests and may be attracted to an area of knowledge without knowing clearly why, their own characterisation of interests must be attended to, but at the same time interrogated.

b   As both General Knowledge Time and Exploration Time are partly to challenge the young people to expand their interests, it is necessary that the students are open to things that they know little about or seldom consider.

c   Although the construction of General Knowledge Time and Exploration Time cannot be bound by the academic subjects, it cannot ignore them entirely either. Academic subjects with their intrinsic values give the opportunity to speak to students in more human-centred terms.

Exploration Time can appear to be fluid and time-consuming, but it is a very important part of the curriculum and the students' learning. We recommend that there be at least two or three sessions each week dedicated to Exploration Time.

Conclusion

The schema for a human-centred curriculum outlined here is motivated by two very important but simple ideas. First, the time that a young person spends at school ought to be enjoyable, balanced and valuable for its own sake. This is because it is not simply a means to an end, that is, a preparation for life as an adult. It is an important part of the young person's present life. This means that time at school should be fun in the broadest sense of the term.

Second, education is aimed at the development of the whole person, and therefore all learning processes are to be holistic. They are a part of his or her personal journey of development. Thus, the educational processes will include all facets of human life and involve the cultivation of relevant qualities or virtues, and these processes will not be limited to the level of knowledge and skills.

This means that the human-centred curriculum will not be constructed around academic subjects as the main organising principle. It means that, insofar as possible, the curriculum and its content will be personalised and structured around the needs of the young person. As we have seen, the major obstacles to self-development that many young people struggle with are those connected to apathy, feelings of disconnection, emotional turmoil and the problems related to relationships with others.

Therefore, the human-centred curriculum will contain time for developing self-awareness, emotional openness and better relationships, as well as stronger cognitive capacities. We refer to this core of the curriculum as the three pillars: mentoring, emotional sharing, and cognitive development. In addition to the triad, there will be time for projects that provide an uninterrupted space for the individual's initiative. There will also be time for exploring new things, as well as time for deepening knowledge in areas that interest the student. These processes require a hub if they are to be personalised in meaningful ways. This hub is the Direction Time with the Mentor. All roads lead back to this hub: the better we can make this time, the better the education of the student will be.

In all of these educational processes, development of the student takes a fundamentally twofold course. On the one hand, it is reaching outwards towards things of value beyond oneself. It is an expansion for the individual. This means that the student becomes more sensitive to, interested in and caring towards other people, society and areas of knowledge. On the other hand, it is reaching inwards towards deeper parts of oneself and towards one's transformation. This requires that the student understands the curriculum as a set of opportunities for self-development.

The overall approach to the curriculum might be better appreciated by reading Chapters 6 and 7 of *Rethinking Secondary Education* (Gill and Thomson, 2012).

In practice, we recognise that any school within the existing system must make compromises in order to embrace a human-centred curriculum as described in this chapter, especially within the constraints of a limited budget and the requirements of the national curriculum. However, this handbook advocates the idea that when students are connected to their learning both inwardly and outwardly through a personalised curriculum, they will be motivated to learn, develop and be willing to turn on their intelligence and be proactive. Once this has happened, the detailed ingredients of the national curriculum will become something well within the students' grasp. In contrast, if this doesn't happen then the national curriculum and its requirements will have no meaning for the student who will then likely tend towards apathy.

Therefore, it is imperative that schools explore creative ways to adapt the practical ideas proposed here to their own situations. For a cohort of students to truly benefit from a human-centred approach, it requires a process of at least three years because it takes time for the teachers and students to understand what these ideas mean in practice within their circumstances. Equally, it takes time for these practices to have meaning for the wider community who may at first be sceptical.

We propose as a first draft the curriculum outlined in Table 3.1 where we have mapped out the human-centred curriculum within a British mainstream school timetable. In this sample curriculum, we have provided two sessions with the Mentor. This is because this is the central hub of the curriculum. One of the two sessions can be dedicated to one-on-one guidance, and the other for a mentor group. Although HCE stresses a personalised timetable for each individual student, it by no means suggests that the school will be in chaos.

Priorities in Table 3.1 are given to the three key pillars of HCE: Direction Time–Group Time–Cognitive Development Time, as well as Independent Project Time and Exploration Time. The latter two curricular elements will provide the student with more engagement time as these are opportunities for their personal development (i.e. knowledge, skills and virtues). All these prioritised curricular elements are rarely seen within a mainstream timetable.

Moreover, in this sample timetable, lunchtime is intentionally longer to offer further opportunities for time out, informal student interactions and socialising. In HCE, such time is as meaningful as time spent studying for subjects.

In the second sample timetable (Table 3.2), we have included traditional subjects which are compulsory within the British national curriculum, such as sciences, English language and literature, mathematics and foreign languages in the spaces allocated as Subject Time.

Similarly, as an illustration of General Knowledge Time, we have proposed topics such as history, geography and religious studies as these are recommended optional subjects (to be taken as GCSEs) in English secondary schools. Furthermore, we have suggested arts, design, music, drama and other creative subjects to be included in the curriculum either as formal subjects to be studied, or as activities for self-exploration.

Table 3.1 Sample weekly timetable

	1	2	3	4	5	6	7	8	9
	08.30–09.00	09.00–9.40	09.45–10.25	10.30–11.10	11.15–11.55	12.00–13.00	13.00–13.40	13.45–14.15	14.20–15.00
Monday	Circle Time	Direction Time	Project Time	Subject Time	Subject Time	Lunch & Socialising	General Knowledge	General Knowledge	Exploration Time
Tuesday	Group Time (peer-led)	Project Time	Subject Time	Subject Time	Subject Time	Lunch & Socialising	Subject Time	General Knowledge	Exploration Time
Wednesday	Group Time	Project Time	Subject Time	Subject Time	Subject Time	Lunch & Socialising	Subject Time	Cognitive Development Time	Exploration Time
Thursday	Group Time (peer-led)	Project Time	Subject Time	Subject Time	Subject Time	Lunch & Socialising	Subject Time	Facilitator-led Group Time	Facilitator-led Group Time
Friday	Direction Time (group)	Project Time	Subject Time	Subject Time	Subject Time	Lunch & Socialising	Subject Time	Cognitive Development Time	Exploration Time

Table 3.2 Sample weekly timetable for an individual student with subjects

	1	2	3	4	5	6	7	8	9
	08.30–09.00	09.00–9.40	09.45–10.25	10.30–11.10	11.15–11.55	12.00–13.00	13.00–13.40	13.45–14.15	14.20–15.00
Monday	Circle Time	Direction Time	Project Time	Mathematics	Foreign Languages	Lunch & Socialising	Religious Studies	History	Activities
Tuesday	Peer-led Group Time	Project Time	English Literature	English Literature	Science	Lunch & Socialising	Mathematics	Geography	Music/Drama Performances
Wednesday	Group Time (Experiential)	Project Time	Science	Science	Arts, Design/Music, Drama	Lunch & Socialising	English	Cognitive Development Time	Sports & Activities
Thursday	Peer-led Group Time	Project Time	Mathematics	English	Science	Lunch & Socialising	Foreign Languages	Group Time (Facilitated)	Group Time (Facilitated)
Friday	Direction Time (group)	Project Time	English	Science	Mathematics	Lunch & Socialising	Foreign Languages	Cognitive Development Time	Activities

Notes

1 Bernstein, B. (1977). *Class codes and control. Vol 3, Towards a theory of educational transmissions.* London: Routledge and Kegan Paul. Bernstein, B. (1990). *The structuring of pedagogic discourse.* London: Routledge.
2 We use the term 'texts' in its broadest sense to include written texts, but also other language events such as lectures, conversations, and so on.
3 Lectures here refer to a broad spectrum of oral presentations in schools, including subject teaching during lessons, for example history, English, geography or sciences; general information presentations; and other presentations such as those given at school assemblies, invited lectures on a specific topic and so forth.

Chapter 4

Human-centred pedagogy

Overview

In this chapter, we describe a human-centred approach to teaching: ways that care, respect, and relationships that underpin teaching. We offer some practical proposals concerning how the teachers can create this kind of learning experience for and with their students. In particular, we discuss in more detail pedagogies for the different proposed curricular elements, and how teaching staff might work together in support of the young person's holistic development.

The key themes discussed in this chapter include

- the teacher's 'role' deconstructed;
- distinct pedagogical activities;
- overall staff relationships.

The curriculum proposals we presented in the previous chapter challenge the conventional conceptions of what it means to be a teacher and to teach. In this chapter, we shall describe how adults in a human-centred school can work together, each playing their respective parts, to facilitate students' learning as holistic development.

In HCE, learning is an activity that is valuable in itself. It may have instrumental value and serve a purpose, but it also has intrinsic or non-instrumental value as an activity that is part of life. The same points apply to teaching. We discuss this aspect of teaching in this chapter and in Chapter 6.

Relationships underpin human-centred pedagogy. Relations are to be understood as an aspect of our communal being rather than as a pedagogical strategy or tool. A person is embedded in a web of relationships, and an adolescent's independence is not detached from these; rather, it exists because of them. Furthermore, good relationships are not merely a means to an end such as for helping students to learn or perform well; they are a fundamental way of being with each other as persons. Therefore, as we saw in Chapter 2, a human-centred school may be understood as a set of relationships.

In a human-centred school, relationships are open and subject to change. They are not merely defined by roles and functions, but also by the fact that people enjoy being together. These relationships are also nurtured by continued dialogue in the community: dialogue about educational culture, flourishing, teaching and learning. Human-centred pedagogy is characterised by sharing at all levels: dialogue between teachers and students, amongst the teaching staff and the management team, between teachers and parents and amongst students themselves. Dialogue helps foster respect and care; it constitutes a way for people to understand and support each other.

The teacher's 'role' deconstructed

As we saw in Chapter 3, in a human-centred curriculum there is no longer a single role of teacher. Because the human-centred curriculum structures the activities and time of the school day around the various needs of students rather than subjects, it separates teaching roles in a way that is quite different from a subject- or discipline-based one. In a similar manner, it dispels the idea that teaching is the professing of a subject matter.

There are five distinct activities that teaching staff carry out to support the students' development:

1   *Mentors* work closely with individual students to help them understand their educational journeys and how these relate to their unique characteristics and life projections.
2   *Group Facilitators* work sensitively with small groups to encourage students to explore, develop and understand their experiences of emotional issues and relationships.
3   *Cognitive Coaches* work closely with small groups of students to help them develop key cognitive capabilities.
4   *Project Supervisors* work one-on-one with students to guide them through the process of designing and implementing their own project work and research inquiry.
5   *Subject/Academic Tutors* teach subject content through lectures, seminars, workshops and other activities.

Ideally, these quite distinct roles require specialist training. For instance, the Mentor role is complex, intense and time-consuming; it will likely require full-time dedication. Furthermore, it entails a set of sensibilities that is quite different from the normal teaching role. In a similar vein, the role of the Facilitator involves specialist abilities that other teachers might not have. Working with young people who are sharing their emotions demands special training. Ideally, we would advocate a similar approach to the work of Cognitive Coach. In an education system that is sensitive to these needs, Cognitive Coaches would receive specialised training specific for their work. In the context of current schools that are resource-stretched, an English or philosophy teacher might take on this task, so long as they can disentangle their new role from their own traditional subject matter or discipline.

In practice, within most state-funded schools in the current system, the same individual might take on several of these distinct teaching activities. As we illustrate below, given the resource constraints of the human-centred school working within a system that isn't human-centred, there are some fruitful and synergetic crossovers between teaching activities. These are important for the school that is trying to become more human-centred. For example, a Subject Tutor of biology can serve as Project Supervisor to any students who are pursuing relevant projects. Similarly, a Cognitive Coach might be a Subject Tutor or Project Supervisor to someone who is doing a writing-intensive project.

However, before we explore these different teaching activities and their possible synergies, we shall first describe some general themes concerning human-centred pedagogy.

Trust

For relationships to flourish within the school community there needs to be trust between all the members. Trust has to be built. It cannot be gained in the short term; it requires long-term relationships. Furthermore, it cannot be acquired instrumentally, solely for the sake of other ends. It needs to be valued for itself and, as such, be part of the culture of the community.

In any school, the nurturing of trust between teachers and students will involve several different kinds of factors. First, at the level of staffing or operation, there will need to be low staff turnover so that students can build lasting relationships with their Mentors, Tutors, and so on. One way to do this is to keep the student with the same Mentors insofar as possible and unless the student requests a change.

Second, at the level of decision-making, it is necessary to engage students in some of the school's decisions, especially those concerning teaching, learning, communal life and well-being. This helps integrate students into the school community, which in turn creates trust.

Third, at the level of ethos the school will have a culture of care, which will generate trust. As we discussed in Chapter 2 ('An overall culture of care'), this culture of caring is vital to engendering trust in a learned community. Everyone contributes to this culture by making caring for others a mutual expectation as well as a reality. In such an environment, for the most part, trust will come naturally. How does one build such a culture? We shall try to answer this question with the next two points.

Fourth, at the level of individual interactions, one develops trust through the content of one's daily exchanges. For example, a culture of trust and caring will preclude certain kinds of malicious gossip and non-constructive criticism. Furthermore, teachers will be proactive in articulating support for students and their holistic development. They will express the understanding that educational processes are for the sake of the development of the young person and they will look out for such learning opportunities for the students. This understanding of education will pervade all interactions. Additionally, the teacher will be proactive in building an emotional ambience conducive to enjoyment and happiness. This might include sharing that lifts the feelings of the group.

Fifth, we can develop trust through the ways in which we communicate. In other words, trust can arise from the manner (rather than just the content) of our communications. Above all, the teachers will be attentive in their listening to students. They should not be quick to interrupt or to assume that they have understood. One can nurture this patient and active listening by appreciating that communication is usually more than an exchange of information. For instance, it is also an opportunity for a young person to express him/herself and perhaps to feel understood. Listening well is a fundamental way to express care and to be sensitive to the needs of students.

Teachers can also embody the values of sensitivity and care in the ways in which they talk to students. For example, one might forgo the opportunity to express annoyance or irritation in the tone of one's voice. Sometimes, teachers unintentionally express paternalism through their choice of words or tone. Sometimes, they express boredom. Teachers can avoid being prematurely and overtly judgemental.

Sixth, key to the development of trust is that a young person should never feel let down or depreciated. It is not easy to predict when a young person will feel let down, especially within the context of closer relationships such as those with a Mentor or Group Facilitator. Therefore, if all teaching staff are sensitive to the state of the students, if a young person feels rejected or let down there are members of staff who can take remedial actions.

General pedagogical activities

Given that there is trust permeating the culture of the school, in general terms we conceive of teaching as consisting of six major types of activity:

1   Creating an environment or a space for learning in which any student would feel safe, cared for, motivated and free from coercion. This space will be one that is conducive to the student's current well-being and happiness.
2   Cultivating students' thirst for understanding and their ability to ask good questions about aspects of the world around them. This is part of the educational process that points motivationally outwards towards the world. The student needs to feel engaged with some areas of knowledge. Often, this aspect of the educational process presents itself as a series of challenges. The self needs to extend its boundaries, and this process starts with questions.
3   Nurturing students' responsibility for their own development, and ultimately for their life. This is part of the educational process that points motivationally inwards, towards the development of the self. Often, this aspect of the educational process manifests itself as a process of self-love or caring for oneself.
4   Challenging students to reflect on their goals and the point of their learning activities. In other words, facilitating a growth in self-conscious awareness concerning their growth with regard to both the outward- and inward-looking processes mentioned above. These distinct processes should come together with regard to the young person's qualities or non-moral virtues. This aspect of the educational process is embodied at the level of virtues.
5   Guiding students on learning pathways by helping them to understand and by setting tasks. This general activity includes liaising and collaborating with other teachers to guide the student on these holistic learning pathways.
6   Reviewing students' learning progress, providing feedback on their learning and helping them determine the next step in their learning journey. This means that educational processes need to be iterative.

In practical terms, we suggest that the school helps each member of the teaching staff to understand his or her responsibility in terms of the above, and review pedagogical practices in terms of these six general activity types.

Another aspect of human-centred pedagogy is that each teacher is a role model for the students. That is to say that they are expected to live human-centred values in their day-to-day practices, including embodying the desirable qualities that an education aims at nurturing in young people such as being generous, sensitive to the needs of others and being self-reflective.

Similarly, teachers must strive to be lifelong learners themselves, not only in their own field of academic knowledge but also in the path of holistic self-development or growth.

Distinct pedagogical activities

In the schematic curriculum outlined in Chapter 3, educational activities are not distinguished primarily in terms of academic subjects. They are defined mainly according to the needs of the young people. This doesn't mean that academic subjects are unimportant. They still have a place in the HCE curriculum, but it is subsidiary to the holistic development of the students.

Because of this, the pedagogical activities carried out by the various teaching staff are quite different. For example, the knowledge, capacities and qualities required of a Mentor differ from those required of a Facilitator, and these vary from those required of a Project Supervisor or Tutor. In the following sections, we will examine each of the roles based on the human-centred curriculum. We suggest that the reader consult the relevant parts of Chapter 3 to better understand each role.

Mentors

A Mentor guides, supports and oversees a student's educational experience and holistic development from the age of 14 onwards throughout the rest of his or her time in secondary education.

There are some essential and desirable qualities and pedagogical virtues that the Mentor should embody.

First, like all human-centred staff, the Mentor will be genuine and authentic in building a close relationship with the students. Such relationships may enable the young person to open up so that they accept support and guidance more readily. In turn, this may help the young person develop a genuine care for his or her own growth and education. The strength of the relationship between the Mentor and the student will determine the quality of the guidance and support that the young person receives. Therefore, this relationship is key to the pedagogy of a human-centred school, which it will prioritise and aim to strengthen.

Second, good Mentors are supportive, caring, patient and empathetic towards the young person. To a certain extent, a Mentor is like a friend or family member to the adolescent within the learning community. However, it is also important to develop this closeness in a professional manner.

Third, Mentors will have a strong understanding of the challenges that adolescents tend to face. They will be sensitive to the particularities of the individual, including his or her attitudes, motivation, talents and interests. For each young person, these can vary from one time to another as they grow and mature. Additionally, the Mentors need to be sensitive to the individual needs of each young person, including known special educational needs (speech and communication, behavioural, mental health, physical, social, emotional and cognitive). These needs will include developmental ones, such as those related to the young person's cognitive capacities, both in the short and medium term. For example, if a student cannot progress because of motivational difficulties, the Mentor will be able to perceive that this is the problem. Or, if a student is having difficulties because of the way they read, then the Mentor will be able to see this. For some students, these kinds of difficulties may appear to be all wrapped up together; in such a case, the Mentor will discern the main roots of the problems.

Finally, these different aspects of the Mentor's work suggest that they will liaise with and consult their colleagues to understand what learning, progress and development mean practically for the student at any time. Mentors have the responsibility to ensure that all efforts to support the young person's learning are well coordinated and integral to their developmental needs. They act as contact hubs amongst the students, other members of the staff, school administrators, professionals from outside agencies and the family and wider community.

In the following sections, we will examine four elements of the Mentor's work.

Getting to know the student

It is important that the Mentor comes to know the young person well. It might be good to start with the student's personal background. As we mentioned in Chapter 3, a life history interview may be a helpful start. Such an interview provides a safe structure for the student to talk about him or herself and life so far, including childhood, and family and friends.

It might also be worthwhile to ask the student to write a brief reflective autobiography, perhaps based on questions such as, 'What do you like most about yourself?' and 'What do you like least about yourself?'

The Mentor needs to know many specifics about the young person in order to be able to guide him or her well. A suitable framework to describe this process might be the three levels of learning which we explained in Chapter 1. These are (1) the cultivation of virtues, (2) the development of skills and (3) the acquisition of knowledge. The more holistic and personal aspects of learning pertains to the virtues. Because such learning is potentially life changing but harder to pin down, it requires a longer-term view of the student's development as a whole person.

The level of the virtues includes the student's motivational attitudes, their capacity to feel self-responsibility and their willingness to connect to issues and knowledge beyond themselves (for instance, to have sustained curiosity and questioning about something). These are all forms of caring. To guide the student, the Mentor needs to take the time to understand the student well, in particular their character, the challenges they face and their weaknesses and strengths in terms of what they care about and how they do so. Are they patient? Do they persevere? What is the person curious about? How do they relate to others? In this way, the Mentor will build up an idea of a holistic development path for the young person, but being careful not to impose false limitations or ideas on them.

At the level of skills, the Mentor will be aware of the student's learning habits and study skills such as those related to time management, prioritising tasks, reducing stress and becoming organised. Good study skills can change a young person's life and deserve to be carefully nurtured. Likewise, the Mentor will need to know the strengths and weaknesses of the student's cognitive capacities and to understand what constitutes progress for the student in this area. He or she will have the insight necessary to help the young person formulate educational goals in this area. For example, the Mentor would be able to recommend that the students work more deeply on their reading skills before thinking about their writing abilities. Once again, improvements in this area will have an important multiplier effect.

The Mentor would try to get to know the student well so that he or she can spot immediate synergistic opportunities that might rapidly take the student to a new level of skills, as well as understanding the student's long-term development, for which progress may occur drop-by-drop.

At the level of knowledge, the Mentor will have a good idea of what the student most needs to learn. This is a difficult judgement call for two reasons. For the first, let us highlight a contrast. On the one hand, we would like to encourage the student to study knowledge disciplines or areas that appeal to their actual motivations or interests, so that they can be more engaged. On the other hand, we want them to take studies that challenge them and expand their horizons. The Mentor needs to know how to reconcile these opposing forces in order to guide the student well. Second, this judgement call requires that the Mentor has a good sense of what is involved in studying all areas of knowledge taught at the school and a positive attitude to the importance of each of them. A Mentor who dislikes the arts or has an aversion to mathematics will be less able to guide students well in these areas.

In terms of knowledge, there are many external constraints on the curriculum because of the national curriculum. Obviously, the Mentor needs to work within these limitations, which means understanding them well. As we have seen, in general terms the human-centred approach to these external constraints is to try to transcend them. If a student has strong virtues and skills then these external requirements such as testing, will seem less of a burden. The challenge is how to help the student lift him or herself to the level at which the tests seem less of a hindrance.

In summary, the Mentor needs to know the young person well. We could summarise this in terms of four steps:

1   getting to know the student's background and personal history (perhaps through a life history interview);
2   understanding the student's character traits (perhaps through a written assignment such as a learning autobiography, as well as through discussions);
3   knowing the student's strengths and weaknesses at each of the levels (virtues, general abilities or skills and knowledge);
4   discovering the student's main interests and passions.

With this knowledge, the Mentor can begin to have an idea of what holistic development paths the student needs for the short, medium and long term. From this knowledge, the Mentor can guide the student in identifying various learning goals.

Setting the context

The Mentor has a very important role in setting the context for the student's educational processes. This can occur in several ways. First, the Mentor can enable the student to understand better what a secondary school education is, and its purpose. In particular, if the student comprehends the ways in which the educational processes of the school will improve one's life then their personal commitment to the learning processes at school will deepen. If it doesn't, then there will be a reason for that, which the Mentor will need to know. For example, if the student is too bothered by other aspects of their life to really care about schooling then this needs to come out. Likewise, if the student feels that their life cannot improve, or feels hopeless then the Mentor ought to know this.

Second, the Mentor can help establish the context for the student with regard to each aspect of the curriculum, but especially those that are challenging or motivationally remote. Too often students don't really understand why they are studying what they study. They merely accept it as a series of imposed chores. This would be quite different in HCE because such understanding is a precondition of engagement and of appreciating the value of learning for its own sake. The primary remedy for disengagement is for the student to co-construct his or her personal curriculum together with the guidance of the Mentor, as we shall see. However, this process of co-construction requires that the student understands the context, that is, the personal meanings, the values and the standards that are implicit in each part of the curriculum. It is part of the Mentor's role to ensure this.

Constructing personalised goals, Learning Agreement and curriculum

We suggest that the Mentor's work, helping the student to construct personal goals, Learning Agreements and curriculum, consists in four steps.

First, the Mentor will help the student articulate a set of goals for the short, medium and long term for their holistic development. These will be focused on the priorities for the student as identified by the student and Mentor together. This means that one would not expect the articulated goals to be complete by any means. The student may well make progress in other areas and achieve things that were not listed in the set of goals.

Second, the two will draw up a Learning Agreement that covers a specified amount of time. This agreement is fundamentally a way for the student to express his or her commitment to personal development in an explicit way. It captures the moment in which the student promises such commitment to him or herself. Through the Learning Agreement, the Mentor would be able to help the student identify areas in which they need to develop holistically. This agreement could be based on the set of learning goals, but it needn't be. The agreement would cover the short, medium and long term.

Third, this agreement might include a learning plan. They will continue to adjust these learning plans, which will evolve as the student's interests develop and their needs become more apparent. These collaborative and self-reflective planning activities will focus on enabling the young person to become more aware of their needs, talents, strengths and shortcomings, and will support their desire to take responsibility for their own development. In other words, the Mentor is aware that the learning plans provide a structure within which the student will connect more fully to the people around them, to the meanings of the learning activities they engage in, and to the content they are learning.

Fourth, the problem now is how to convert the goals, agreement and plan into what the student does each day. The Mentor will guide the student in constructing a personalised curriculum which includes all the curricular elements outlined in Chapter 3, but which is also based on the courses and workshops that the school offers. The Mentor and student will work together and 'translate' the learning goals into a personalised, timetable. Although the courses on offer are common to many, this doesn't mean that each student cannot have a highly personalised schedule to attain their goals.

The Mentor will ensure that the student understands how their weekly schedule of activities fits into their overall development. With this in mind, the Mentor and the student can begin to map the elements of the Learning Agreement to a possible curriculum and schedule. This mapping shouldn't be mechanical. In the process of mapping, there may well unfold important aspects of the student's educational process that aren't written down in the Learning Agreement. For this reason, the mapping may involve some shift of priorities.

Nurturing and challenging

In Chapter 3, we discussed that the personalised curriculum must be at once nurturing and challenging.

It is a precondition of its being nurturing that the Mentor is sensitive to the outward (being motivated to pursue learning for its own sake) and inward (e.g. being motivated to connect one's learning experience to one's life) processes that the student undergoes. For this reason, one of the key responsibilities of a Mentor is to guide the young person towards feeling motivated and wanting to be responsible for their own development and life. Nurturing begins with motivation. The Mentor will be especially attentive to ways in which the student relates to the learning process as something valuable and enjoyable for its own sake. What areas of knowledge do they connect to, and why? What areas of knowledge do they not connect to, and why not? Equally, the Mentor will be perceptive to ways in which the student understands the importance of learning for their life. Does he or she see these learning processes as vital for their own development and future? How can such feelings and understanding be strengthened, deepened and nourished?

In addition, the Mentor must be able to challenge the student in ways that are constructive and meaningful, such as posing questions at the right time, or encouraging the student to consider goals that they have never dared to consider before. These challenges may often have an emotional aspect to them, especially when students have low self-esteem and expectations of themselves. For instance, the challenge is to not only complete a difficult piece of mathematics or complete a project, but also for the student to reframe his or her self-perception.

Supporting the student's holistic development

In order to support the student's development and to pinpoint the obstacles that he or she faces – whether cognitive, emotional or motivational – the Mentor must know the student well.

With regard to the cognitive obstacles, the Mentor will discuss a diagnosis with the student, which can be used to construct the programme for their Cognitive Development Time. The deeper and better the diagnosis, the more directly the training can help the student to overcome these obstacles so that their intelligence can become more alive and active.

If a student suffers from major motivational and emotional obstacles, such as anxiety, low self-esteem or emotional conflicts with family, this can result in their lacking motivation and finding education meaningless. To overcome these issues, the Mentor provides more focused individual support to the student. This takes time, coordination and collaboration. It may include identifying when students require support from other professionals and different agencies, and liaising with them to ensure that there is a system of appropriate support, especially for students with special educational needs and for students from disadvantaged backgrounds.

The Mentor will help the student identify their main interests in life; a young person might not know what they are interested in. Also, their knowledge of the options may be limited; they might find it difficult to separate whims and enduring interests. So, conversations about these interests will help the young person gradually piece together a picture of his or her interests, talents and possible life trajectories. The Mentor mainly just listens and asks questions. In this process, it is important that the Mentor not be quick and judgemental. We don't want students to close down their possibilities early in life. Yet, the opportunity for the student to begin to articulate the possible shape of his or her future will help to make the student more self-aware.

Providing feedback

Another role of the Mentor is to provide feedback to the student on their development and learning, and to review the student's progress. This requires that the Mentor understands well what counts as progress in different academic subject areas, as well as more broadly in terms of personal and cognitive development. It also means that the Mentor has relevant feedback from the other teachers.

Connected to the learning feedback and review, Mentors will help the student prepare learning portfolios (more on this in Chapter 5), which represent the young person's progress. This not only provides an overview of the student's learning journey and of her development, but it also celebrates her learning. A personalised record of the student's progress would be collated by the student, which might be used as part of the student's portfolio to be presented to higher educational institutions or potential employers.

Group Facilitators

Ideally, the Facilitators of Group Time would be professionals who are trained in facilitating group sessions in which young people share their experiences and feelings with their peers. The central task of the Facilitator is to build a safe, confidential and open space in which the young people can share without fear. The Facilitator constructs the culture of these meetings.

The main aim of the session is for young people to share their feelings and emotions with each other. This will provide an opportunity for them to understand their own feelings and emotions better as well as those of others' better. It also helps young people learn how to relate to each other better, including romantic relationships, within the context of an agreed code of ethics.

An important quality that a Facilitator needs is the ability to listen with care and be sensitive to emotional needs. He or she should also have the ability to hold together meetings that might be emotionally charged, to manage group dynamics and to defuse potentially violent and emotionally intense outbursts.

Like Mentors, Facilitators care for young people: they are friendly, patient, approachable and personable, and their manner and attitudes will support trusting relationships. The Facilitator ensures that all students feel supported and protected by the environment of the group, and that they are nurtured through the process of working through difficult issues. When the need arises, the Facilitator will also provide individual counselling support. The Facilitator will be prepared to continue to support a student beyond the allocated Group Time if their professional judgement deems this necessary. It may be that issues or concerns arise in Group Time which the Facilitator may feel are beyond the abilities of a group to deal with. In these cases, they would ask the student(s) involved to speak with them privately and would follow appropriate child-protection procedures. All Facilitators will have access to professional supervision for themselves.

For each group session, the Facilitator plans possible activities. However, while being sensitive to the group's needs, he or she will be prepared to improvise when departing from the plan seems appropriate. As we touched on in Chapter 3, Group Time will include some specific sessions for open-ended, student-led discussions and for explorations of them; the Facilitator will integrate the themes arising from these conversations into meaningful learning experiences for the whole group.

The Facilitator won't underestimate the value of simply allowing young people to talk about and reflect on their experiences in a safe space. Group Time is not intended to be therapy; rather, it provides a fertile safe space for young people to share their feelings and emotions and to reflect on their relationships with others.

Cognitive Coaches

The work of Cognitive Coaches is to provide each student with the opportunity to develop cognitively but free from the additional requirements of any discipline or traditional subject. This is time for the young person to expand, strengthen and deepen the use of their intelligence. The aim is to take the student's overall learning capacities to a new level.

Preparation

It is very important that the students approach cognitive training with the right attitude: the more they want to develop and feel ready to engage with the process, the better. Such a desire will arise from students understanding that Cognitive Development Time is dedicated to them, that it is a unique opportunity and that having strong cognitive capacities may transform their lives. Some students may not want to engage with the process because of lack of confidence. Others may be reluctant to engage in the process because they are generally passive and turned off.

To take the student to a new level in their capacity to learn, the programme needs to be personalised insofar as possible. There is no point in making a young person work through exercises in a routine way if there is a more fundamental obstacle to be overcome. For example, if a student attends to what they are reading then there is no point in helping them with more advanced comprehension skills.

This means that the Cognitive Coach needs a keen and sympathetic eye for the major factors that impede a student. Likewise, if the coach is sensitive then he or she will be aware of the contexts in which a young person shows an intelligence that is alive and bright, and of the times when it is less so. This will help the coach to encourage the student to be more engaged and proactive. A Cognitive Coach might employ established cognitive tests to establish how the students are doing.

Cognitive Coaches will liaise with other members of staff, especially with the Mentors, about each student's needs, problems and progress. If the Cognitive Coaches are also Subject Tutors, they will need to juxtapose their different responsibilities.

The process

As we indicated in the curriculum section, there needs to be a staggered approach towards the development of cognitive skills. In this way, it is comparable to learning a musical instrument: we start with basic skills and move towards more complex ones. However, the good Cognitive Coach will be aware of the whole state of the student and will adapt the approach to the condition of the student. For example, students who are mentally alert but undisciplined and easily bored will need a quite different approach from the student who doesn't think much for him or herself but is very meticulous in what they do.

Although the content of the programme is largely focused on the development of high-level cognitive *skills*, such as reading, listening, talking, writing and reasoning, nevertheless, the programme also addresses the student's intellectual *virtues*. Broadly, we can divide these into those that concern how attention is pointed outwards, and those that are self-regarding. The first concerns how one cares for what motivates an inquiry. Let us consider some general examples: a person who studies the life cycle of a moth will care about how these moths live; a historian will care about the period of the past she is studying. In general, the person cares for the thing she is studying. More specifically, in some contexts, being accurate regarding detailed data is more important than being critical; in other circumstances, it is more important to have a systematic overview than to be strategically focused on one point. A person's capacity to sense such differences depends on their caring about the truth in relevant ways.

Second, self-regarding intellectual virtues are dispositions to care about the ways in which one knows or believes. For example, some readers are caught up in detail and cannot see the bigger panorama, while others don't pay much attention to detail because they become impatient quickly. Some people punish themselves when they make a mistake; others are less critical of themselves. The main point is that the Cognitive Coaches understand that the process of the students is not only at the level of skills; it also involves their intellectual virtues, which is their capacity to care.

Other points

Since Cognitive Development Time is supposed to have a very different flavour from usual class time, we would recommend that these sessions not be conducted in a standard classroom. We hope that the atmosphere would be more personal and friendly, more direct in its care for the individual.

Cognitive Coaches may have backgrounds in a variety of disciplines including linguistics, philosophy, mathematics or sciences. They will recognise that cognitive capacities go beyond the conventional 'study skills' and that, in fact, these capacities form part of the person as a whole and require the internalisation of epistemological values.

Part of Cognitive Development Time may be dedicated to conversations and discussions. This means that the Cognitive Coaches must have the ability to create spaces for such dialogues and to cultivate the appropriate classroom dynamics.

To summarise: in conjunction with the Direction Time and Group Time, the Cognitive Development Time will provide an extra boost to students' capacities and willingness to learn in the broad sense of the term. If successful, this threefold process of development will take the student to a new plane in their whole-person learning. Time spent on these more personal processes will enable more students to engage with their learning meaningfully. In the medium term, this will change the *ethos* of the school so that it becomes more of a learning community. This means that the culture will be one in which people express more care for each other, and that the community will be happier.

Project Supervisors

A Project Supervisor (hereafter 'Supervisor') facilitates and oversees students' independent projects. The main aim of this time is to provide a space for students to work directly on areas of knowledge or questions that they care about and to have a greater ownership of the learning process. Supervisors are generally also Academic Tutors and subject specialists, but they have additional training in project supervision aimed at cultivating students' independence in project work.

Choosing an area

In collaboration with the Mentor, a Supervisor will guide the student in clarifying their topic of interest. In general, the Mentor usually helps the student choose a general area to work on; the Supervisor helps the student turn this into a manageable project.

Both the Mentor and Supervisor will be sensitive to the challenges that students encounter in choosing their projects. For instance, a young person may not be good at identifying what they are interested in. They might be tempted to focus on short-term whims rather than longer-term interests. They may be unaware of areas of knowledge that might engage them. Additionally, a student might limit their project due to a lack of confidence, or because of an unvoiced feeling that certain topics are not appropriate for them. For all of these reasons, it is worth spending time on the process of clarification because if the general topic is well chosen then the project potentially can change a young person's life.

Likewise, it is important that the topic be transmuted into a question or set of questions that will challenge the student in ways that are appropriate. The process of turning a topic into a set of questions will involve the student, so his or her feeling of ownership and personal meaningfulness is not harmed.

For older students, it may be better to have a project that lasts a whole year; for the younger ones, a project that lasts a term may be better. For students in between, it may be better to conceive of two related projects, each lasting a term or semester.

All of these points mean that the process of defining the project needs to involve the Mentor as well as the student and the Supervisor. This is mainly because the Mentor will know the student better and have a better grasp of what learning opportunities the project needs to provide. However, Supervisors will be involved in the genesis of the project, especially towards the later stages of the process. This is because they will have more experience in the art of guiding students towards a successful project.

Defining a question and formulating a plan

Once a general project area has been chosen, the Supervisor needs to help the student define a set of questions that will be answered through the project. This will form the basis of the project's plan.

Some students will need more guidance in this second stage of formulating questions and structuring a plan. Others will feel that such guidance is an intrusion and will need a gentle touch. For individual projects, the Supervisor will question the student's ideas and challenge their project design or approach, albeit in a constructive and supportive manner. The Supervisor will ensure that the student keeps a good balance: on the one hand, they will avoid recycling material from previous classes; on the other, they will avert unintentionally foreshadowing material from later in the year.

The project plan will get to the heart of a student's most enduring interests. In helping the student select the questions and plan the project, the Supervisor will also help ensure that the project is appropriately challenging for the student. It should also signal the relevant methodology for the area of inquiry.

If the Supervisor feels that there is another member of staff more qualified to help with the framing of a project, then he or she should set up a one-on-one tutorial or a three-way conversation between the student, the Supervisor and the specialist Tutor.

The project process

To enable students to engage meaningfully in the project process, Supervisors need to have a good understanding of the challenges that the student will face and the standards to be achieved.

First, Supervisors will understand the challenges and obstacles that a young person will likely encounter. This will include being more organised, seeking and selecting information from diverse sources and (when relevant) analysing data. In this process, the Supervisor will guide the student towards greater self-reliance.

The Supervisor will help the student build connections between the project work and their learning and growth. As with other areas of learning, the project process points both outwards and inwards. Regarding the first, the student will be robustly connected to the meaningful nature of the subject area; he or she will regard the project as something interesting and worthwhile. Concerning the second, the inwards-pointing process, the student will sense that this is an opportunity for them to develop and grow, to strengthen their capacities. The Supervisor will facilitate both of these processes.

Second, Supervisors will understand well the standards that define progress in independent inquiries. They will help the student appreciate what counts as a good complete project and facilitate their taking the necessary steps to realise the project accordingly. Supervisors will be familiar with the standards to provide feedback during the project and to review, with the student, where the project stands from a holistic perspective. During these reviews, the Supervisor will help the student to make critical decisions in relation to achieving the project's aims, and will challenge them to take the project further.

Supervisors might facilitate discussions about the subject area with other students who are working on projects within a similar field. This creates opportunities for peer support.

Additionally, Supervisors are aware that independent projects can vary greatly and can often morph substantially during the process. This means that they will be open to liaising with other staff to find appropriate support for a student, if this becomes necessary.

The project review

Whether the student has completed a term-long or a year-long project, there will be a final review process. This might involve, for instance, a presentation, an oral examination and/or an interview that includes some self-assessment and reflection by the student. This will not only bring closure to a process that hopefully enables the student to feel pride in their achievement, but will also encourage them to apply the learning to ongoing project work or to new ventures.

Subject/Academic Tutor

A Subject/Academic Tutor (hereafter 'Tutor') is someone who is trained in a particular academic discipline such as one of the natural sciences, humanities, social studies or business studies. Tutors tend to cover a more diverse range of curricular elements than the Mentors, Cognitive Coaches and Facilitators. They will work with students during Specialist Subject Time, General Knowledge Time and Exploration Time, as well as during the time slots allocated for projects. Therefore, for the Tutor teaching can take a number of forms:

- lectures and seminars to introduce general knowledge within a particular field and help equip students with appropriate knowledge about certain subjects; some of these lectures would be part of the young person's development in general knowledge and others would be part of their exploration;
- lectures and seminars for understanding, reflecting, learning and questioning on specific topics within a subject area; these sessions are related to the student's special Subject Time and perhaps to some individual projects;
- one-on-one supervision on the student's project progress;
- providing regular feedback and periodical review of the student's progress;
- tutoring and training students to successfully take part in public exams.

Human-centred education regards the young person's holistic development as the core value. This core value will modulate the pedagogy of the teaching of standard subjects. That is to say, a human-centred approach isn't simply a normal school curriculum laced with additional activities or programmes such as Cognitive Development Time and Group Time. It is definitely not the traditional school approach with an added layer on top. Instead, it is a transformation of the whole system.

This implies that the Tutors face three challenges. The first is adapting the teaching of their specialist knowledge to the human-centred approach. What does this mean in practice? The second challenge arises because they have less time in the curriculum for teaching their own area of knowledge. Will they feel the need to cram more knowledge into less time? How do they ensure that learning is not diluted? The third is to prepare the young people for the public exams within this more limited time period and without making it the goal of learning.

Adapting specialist knowledge

With regard to the first challenge, there are two ideas that might help the Tutors to adapt. The HCE's central concern means that the pedagogy has to be centred on the question: 'How can teaching a particular discipline contribute, in part, to the development of the young people?'

As we emphasised earlier, the idea that a person's development pointing both outwards and inwards provides a useful framework. Let's apply it to subject learning:

- *Outwardly*: Primarily, the student needs to connect meaningfully to the intrinsic value of the discipline, to the subject matter as such and for its own sake. For instance, in the case of history, the student should connect to what is meaningful and fascinating about the past, or in the case of biology, to what is interesting about the life of plants. Knowledge is always an answer to a set of questions and its meanings are defined by those questions. Therefore, Tutors will help students find their way into the kinds of questions that motivate a discipline. The more this can happen, the more engaged with the subject the student will be. Without it, the study will have little meaning for the student. Moreover, the student must connect meaningfully to the values of the discipline. The Tutor will help the student to internalise the epistemological values that are inherent in the discipline. For example, such values are inherent in the scientific method or textual interpretation or sensitivity to language use.
- *Inwardly*: Part of the student's development is to become more self-aware within the confines set by the curriculum. For example, Tutors can offer the student the opportunity to apply and hone cognitive skills such as critical thinking. When the student comes to recognise that this is what she is doing and understands its importance, she has become more self-aware of her development. In a similar fashion, during General Knowledge Time, the Tutor can help the student connect different areas of knowledge. In a similar vein, during Exploration Time, Tutors create the space for the student to expand their horizons.

As already discussed, the development of the young person occurs at three levels: knowledge, skills and virtues. The way knowledge is learned is very important. For example, when a student is curious and when they have the skills to learn then they will. In contrast, force-fed knowledge seldom leads to the development of higher-level skills and the kinds of sensitivities and caring that the intellectual virtues require. Therefore, the appropriate pedagogy cannot be based simply on knowledge learning. It needs to lead quickly to the development of skills and the cultivation of virtues that are meaningful to the student on their own terms. It would be a mistake to think of skills only as the ability to manipulate information or the expertise to do something well. It also includes the ability to enter into the concepts of a discipline. The learning of appropriate skills will include the understanding of the main concepts of a discipline. How the teacher might do this will be a topic of Chapter 6.

Coping with time pressures in schools

The second challenge concerns the pressures of time in schools, specifically the anxiety that not enough time will be put into subject teaching in a human-centred curriculum. Although it may not appear this way at first, the human-centred approach is aimed at relieving these time pressures. The idea is that the teachers focus predominantly on what really matters: the holistic development of the young person. There has to be time for this.

The illusion that there isn't time can be dispelled by examining three points. First, perhaps one can recognise and feel that there is time, once one gives up on the assumption that students need to be forced into acquiring knowledge that has and will have no meaning for them. As a teacher, if one feels that one's job is primarily to enable every student to learn a whole curriculum of knowledge given certain external academic standards, then one is constantly working against the clock. The point of the human-centred approach to the curriculum is to remove the assumption that this is the primary role of every teacher.

Instead, HCE organises the curriculum according to student needs rather than according to academic subjects. This constitutes a reframing of the academic in terms of personal development. What becomes urgent isn't the knowledge as such, but rather the need for the psychological and cultural conditions that would make such knowledge meaningful for the student. For this reason, as we have seen, the parts of the curriculum oriented towards knowledge learning are divided into Specialist Subject Time, General Knowledge Time and Exploration Time. This permits students to acquire concepts and knowledge according to their interests and needs. It is better for a young person to have a rudimentary knowledge and understanding of a subject but which means something to them, than to go through a long course on the same subject that means very little to them.

The second point is that the human-centred approach aims to take the student to a new level. It invests time in the transformation of the person. It doesn't do this for the sake of academic performance. Nevertheless, if the student is improving and developing then in general this will yield better academic results. In a sense, the idea of HCE is to treat the causes rather than the symptoms. If a young person is not interested in learning, even in the broad sense of the term, then the school needs to find the underlying reasons for this and work with him so that he can improve himself.

Third, in the existing system the responsibility for the overall development of the students lies with the class teachers. In effect, this combines all of the roles described here into one. In a traditional school, the teacher implicitly acts like Mentor, Facilitator, Coach and Supervisor, as well as Tutor. Furthermore, not only are these roles combined in one person, but also this is done in a setting that makes their fulfilment very difficult. In a traditional school with classes of thirty students and above and with few opportunities to get to know students well, it is very difficult for a teacher to help individual students develop significantly. The traditional school seems to be designed for exam results. In sharp contrast, in HCE the system is designed for the development of the person. This means that the roles of Mentor, Coach, Facilitator and Supervisor are not combined into one. The overall responsibility for enabling the student to develop lies primarily with the Mentor (well, actually, it belongs to the student). In this way, the Tutors can feel that their work is more specific and hopefully less pressurised than that of a traditional teacher, who in a sense has to do everything. Furthermore, the process of enabling the student to develop holistically does not occur in a traditional classroom setting.

Dealing with the pressures of preparing for exams

The third challenge is that Tutors need to prepare and train the student to pass public exams.

It is important for the reader to understand that the human-centred approach to education advocates fundamental changes to the educational system as a whole and thus, to the way that schools, curriculums and assessment are conceived. In Chapter 9 of the book *Rethinking Secondary Education: A Human-Centred Approach* (Gill and Thomson, 2012), we argue that an educational system does *not* have to be focused on public exams that result in grades. The kinds of information that employers, other educational institutions and governments need don't have to be combined in one grading system.

However, the human-centred approach can be applied at the level of the educational system, the institution and the individual. In this handbook, we are concerned primarily with what HCE means at the institutional level, that is, for schools. In other words, in this context one must work within the system, even though one might also argue that it needs changing.

In a human-centred school, doing well in public exams would not be the focus of the student's learning . At the same time, HCE does value the need for qualifications through taking part in public exams. The question remains: 'How can we prepare the student to do well in these exams given that much of the curriculum is devoted to other things?'

In a way, the answer to this question has already been given. The HCE approach tries to deal with the underlying causes rather than the symptoms. Given the student's cognitive development, greater emotional maturity, growth in self-awareness and greater independence through project work, there is good reason to think that most students will be on a new level in terms of their development. Therefore, they should be better prepared for the exams in a deeper sense than simply knowing the required information and having the relevant competencies. Thus, the Tutors can take two to three terms helping the student to understand the nature of the exams in each subject, what counts as a good standard exam paper and what it takes to achieve good results. For students who desire to be high achievers in exams, the Tutors can help them fulfil their aspirations.

Overall staff relationships

So far, we have examined pedagogies for the different curricular elements and looked at how teachers might work together in support of the young person's holistic development.

Needless to say, a HCE that promotes care, respect and relationships will desire the same amongst all members of staff in a school.

Because of this, a human-centred school should dedicate substantial time to enable staff members to engage with one another and teachers in meaningful conversations. In doing so, the staff team can model the human-centred relationships with all members of the school community, including the students and parents. There will be opportunities for staff to meet in an open, unstructured way every week to discuss teaching and other school topics.

Mentors will liaise on a regular basis with other staff members, not least of course with the Facilitators, Cognitive Coaches, Supervisors and Tutors. Weekly meetings are important for the team to come together to exchange teaching experiences, reflect on individual students' learning and progress and discuss ways to help them. It is during such team meetings that discussions about strategies take place so that they can be implemented in ways to ensure integrated and coherent support to each individual student. It is always helpful when key concerns and positive observations and suggestions arising in staff conversations are appropriately recorded or documented, to allow for monitoring of progress and to help the staff to recall the detail of each individual's learning needs.

Conclusion

Throughout this handbook, we have highlighted that the central concern of teaching is the well-being and holistic development of the student as a human being. This means that human-centred pedagogy respects the young person who needs guidance, feedback, challenges and support from a caring teacher. It recognises the adolescent's need for independence as well as the necessity for teachers to cultivate their capacities for taking responsibility for their own learning. Growth needs both internal push and external pull. Thus, by focusing on the well-being and holistic development of the person, teaching can avoid both the coercive pursuit of academic subject knowledge and the romantic idea of non-interference.

In HCE, we deconstruct the conventional multifaceted roles of the monolithic teacher and point out that no one teacher can perform so many different roles well at the same time. Instead, we conceive of teaching as a partnership and collaboration amongst many professionals, who together can facilitate and guide the young person's learning.

Common amongst all the teaching staff are such qualities as: genuine care for the young person; a dedication and capacity to build positive human relations with the students; professional qualifications and knowledge; a profound understanding of what learning is; and a love for learning. It goes without saying that there are other qualities that are equally desirable, including a sense of humour, patience, friendliness, firmness and the ability to make learning an engaging experience for all.

Another aspect of teaching is connected with teachers' own learning at both personal and professional levels. This is linked to the school's capacity to nurture teachers' growth and provide spaces for ongoing reflection on teaching practices and teachers' own learning. This will be one of the topics of Chapter 6 on teacher training.

Chapter 5

Human-centred approach to educational evaluation

Overview

In this chapter, we distinguish the different purposes and needs for review and evaluation and point out the critical error of lumping them under the umbrella word 'assessment'. In doing so, we make it clear that when education is overly dominated by the demand for performing well in high-stake exams, it can only offer something narrow, hollow and superficial for the students, and equally, it makes the teachers' work onerous and stressful. The main part of this chapter provides general guidelines using case studies and examples of meaningful alternatives that schools can adopt to replace over reliance on testing and exams. These include learning feedback, learning review, portfolios and exhibitions.

The key themes discussed in this chapter are:

- feedback for students;
- feedback for teachers;
- learning review;
- portfolios.

Before we explain a human-centred approach to assessment within schools, a broader discussion about assessment in general is needed.

Assessment in education refers to a process of making judgements about students' learning based on the evidence that educational authorities consider valid and important, including how this evidence is collected, and equally, how it is interpreted. Currently, educational assessment is divided into two kinds: formative assessment, which is supposed to help students to learn better, and summative assessment consisting in testing and grading, which judges what the students have learned and how well they have mastered the curriculum content and expectations.

In the current educational system it is easy for educational processes to become little more than the means to attaining good grades in public exams. In Gill and Thomson (2012), we showed why this is a profound mistake. In summary, testing and grades are problematic in three ways.

First, exams are harmful insofar as they become the main goal of the student (and increasingly, of the teacher and the school as a whole and hence, the culture of the institution). In this way, learning becomes instrumentalised and its real value becomes replaced by its measurement. This is pernicious because it prevents students from appreciating and connecting to the intrinsic value of their learning processes. When learning becomes for the sake of a grade, testing drains it of its value.

Second, achieving good exam results comes to be regarded like money and in this sense, the results become regarded not as a measurement or representation of something real and valuable, but rather as something real and valuable themselves. They become goals of instrumental value merely because they are perceived as such by society. It is an unfortunate self-fulfilling prophecy. It is a collective illusion by which the measurement replaces the real thing.

Third, preparation for exams tends to be focused on learning at the knowledge level; the priority of the other levels is ipso facto ignored. In other words, the real meaning of learning is bypassed.

Indeed, grades tend to be discouraging and unkind. They do not send the right message about learning, nor do they help review where the student is in relationship to their personal goals and progress. Furthermore, when exams and grades are used not only to judge students' learning, but to judge how well a school has been teaching the curriculum content, this 'evidence' is often regarded as the reference for deciding whether to award a school or punish it, which in the worst case can be the closing of a school. Hence, testing is often referred to as 'high stakes'. High-stakes testing thus puts huge pressure on school leaders and teachers whose focus is increasingly to improve test results, and such pressure is in turn transferred to students who are made to believe that if they haven't done well enough in their exams, they are de facto failures. Hence, teachers are teaching to test, students are learning to pass tests, and the school's leadership and governance becomes solely focused on increasing test scores – a vicious cycle.

In order to offer pointers towards an alternative system that avoids these mistakes, we separate five very different informational purposes that assessment or evaluation is supposed to serve:

1   to help students improve educationally;
2   to help teachers better support students' development;
3   to provide employers with information about the student as a candidate for a job or a vocational training programme, such as an apprenticeship;
4   to provide other educational institutions (further education and higher education) with information about the student as a candidate for apprenticeship or further study;
5   to provide the government (and parents and taxpayers) with information about the school's educational standards for the sake of accountability.

We argue that these five purposes should not be grouped under one single category of 'assessment' as they are in the current testing system. In effect, the current system makes evaluation needs that are an integral part of the educational process of young people (i.e. 1, 2) hostage to informational needs that are external and inimical to that process (i.e. 3, 4 and 5). This is what tends to instrumentalise education. Trying to serve all five purposes at once through exams and grades may appear efficient, but it constitutes a systemic failure to respect young people because it involves testing them for the sake of ends that are not theirs. Furthermore, it does so in a way that damages their real ends and destroys the meaning of the educative processes.

Additionally, it is not necessary for these five kinds of purposes to be combined. They are indeed very different and, therefore, should be served by different procedures. The idea that they can and ought to be kept separate should strike one as a liberating idea because it allows each requirement to be considered on its own merits.

The position that we have just outlined argues for a fundamental change in the educational system. Human-centred education attempts to re-envisage the very institution of a secondary school, and therefore in this chapter we propose alternatives to assessment within a school's confines.

As already indicated, the real focus of assessment and evaluation within schools should be on helping students improve their learning experiences, enabling them to achieve their goals and ensuring that they partake in responsibility for their own development. It is clear that this requires different approaches to testing and grades.

Therefore, this chapter is structured as follows. First, we characterise the general nature of learning feedback for students within a human-centred approach. Second, we look at feedback for teachers who will need such information and evaluation in order to provide the appropriate support for each student. Third, we present a suggestion for a human-centred approach to student learning review, and describe a possible model of learning review that may be integrated into the curriculum proposals of Chapter 3. Last, we offer some practical examples illustrating how a human-centred approach to learning review can ensure a central focus on improving students' learning experiences, qualities and overall goals.

Feedback for students

In HCE, feedback is an integral part of the student's learning and developmental process. It is vital that the Mentors, Facilitators, Coaches and Tutors not only reflect with the student on their progress but also liaise with each other so as to give the student consistent feedback.

Feedback for students has two essential features. First, it exemplifies the idea that students are responsible for their own learning. Second, it embodies the principle that such learning consists in the student's holistic development. From these two primary features, a couple of other points follow. Third, it requires that the student understands the relevant standards well. That is to say that the process of providing feedback is one of helping the student understand better what counts as good and better, and why. However, what counts as improvement depends in part on the student's own goals which are defined in collaboration with the Mentor, and such improvement must be holistic. It cannot be merely academic in the normal sense of the word. It will include the development of character, disposition and other personal qualities. Fourth, because such feedback is part of the learning process, it is non-judgemental. It ought to be loving, generous and usually gentle because such qualities are fundamental for the student to improve him or herself and his or her learning. Such feedback doesn't consist in a grade that encourages the student to compare herself to others. It is different from a grade in that what is important is the content of the feedback. It is a set of messages. Furthermore, it encourages the student to improve relative to his or her own past (relative to a set of standards or criteria) rather than to become better than someone else. In this way, it should embody and require critical self-reflection.

It may be helpful to think of such feedback as being addressed at four levels.

At the first level, there is feedback pertaining to specific projects or tasks. Such task-based feedback should be timely, focusing on giving very practical advice in terms of the strengths of the student's work, and suggestions with regard to the ways she might improve the quality of her project or task. Some feedback is immediate and can take place during the class conversation or be given in the form of written comments about the student's work. It is not judgemental and is more informative than a grade, and can help the student improve the quality of her work.

Second, feedback should be given to the student on her learning processes and approach to learning. This feedback is based on an overview of the student's learning journey over a period of time, and the ways that he is able to take responsibility and care for her learning experience. The emphasis of such feedback is on enhancing the student's abilities and approaches to understanding.

Feedback at these two levels will often come from a Project Supervisor, or Tutor.

At the third level, the young person will receive feedback on her commitment, self-control and confidence. Such feedback is connected to how learning supports the cultivation of personal qualities and caring dispositions and, therefore, will most likely be provided by the Mentor.

Finally, the student needs feedback on the overall development of herself as a person. Once again, such advice is often provided by a Mentor who knows the student well, including her interests, priorities and personal trajectories.

Feedback at the last two levels is helpful for reviewing where the student is in light of her short-, medium- and long-term goals and overall learning.

If students do require comparative feedback on their work, then we might try alternative tacks. For example, suppose that a student has written a paper and receives detailed comments on what aspects of his work could be improved, how and why. The feedback function is to give him a general comparative idea of how well he has done, not in relation to other students, but rather in relation to certain standards. This feedback needs to be given in a manner that is less judgemental and more informative (not one-dimensional) than a single grade. One might, for example, provide the students with anonymous high-quality essays written by other students on a similar topic, which could then be analysed with the group. In this way, students learn more about the qualities in the writing that they need to develop, and about what counts as improvement in this context and why.

An alternative approach is to encourage more active self-evaluation in terms of the student's own past, ipsative feedback. Questions to reflect on include 'How have I improved in X since last month?' or, 'How could I improve more?'

Feedback for teachers

Teachers need information about how their students are progressing in order to be able to adjust what and how they *teach,* and to better understand the learning needs of their students, individually and as a group. In this light, teachers need feedback about how well they are working.

The trouble is that we tend to think of student needs at the level of knowledge rather than in terms of concepts, skills and qualities, or more holistically. This is due to the word 'teach'. Teachers who are trained in a specific subject area may assume that teaching consists primarily in imparting knowledge (and some skills) within a discipline. This kind of assumption narrows our understanding of 'teaching' and it is problematic. Learning should be a holistic process of development, which includes qualities, skills and concepts as well as knowledge. Well-motivated students with a reasonable dose of common sense can often acquire much knowledge without the help of a teacher. For instance, some students can easily grasp factual knowledge through reading or collecting information on the Internet. The immediate availability of information and factual resources makes a certain kind of teaching totally redundant.

Revisiting these points (already highlighted in Chapter 4) helps us to redefine the kind of feedback that teachers need (about their students) in order to support students' holistic development. For HCE, the two key concerns are that the young person feels happy with his or her life at the school, and that the young person feels motivated and connected to what they are doing at the school. In this way, the student can begin to feel the responsibility for his or her own learning or holistic development. This means that the student needs to understand the value of what he or she is doing in the school and how it connects to their overall development as a person. In this manner, the student can engage more directly with identifying their learning trajectories. Ongoing feedback enables them to reflect on their experience in education and use such reflection to guide further learning. In these different ways, the feedback that a teacher needs concerns primarily the overall development of the student and, only in this context, more specific feedback related to particular projects and tasks.

The feedback must be appropriate for the part that the teacher plays in the student's education. As we have already explained, a human-centred approach dissolves the single block concept of the teacher and replaces it with that of Mentor, Coach, Advisor, Specialist Tutor and so forth. Each of them has different feedback needs, which require teachers to collaborate with one another in sharing their understanding of the student's progress. This is achieved through the coordination of the Mentor. This means that during the team meetings, a good portion of time will be allocated to teachers sharing their feedback on individual students. (For more detail about collaboration between the different roles, see Chapter 4.)

Teachers need feedback for a second reason: feedback on their own ability to facilitate and strengthen the development of the student. This kind of feedback is very different from judgement pertaining to professional development or reflection on practice.[1]

As an antidote, the whole idea of assessment needs to be abandoned in favour of feedback for teachers, which would be an integral part of their teaching activities. Feedback can help teachers in their various teaching positions, rather than assess them on their ability to enhance students' exam results. Once again, feedback for teachers shouldn't be focused at the level of their ability to impart knowledge, although in some situations, such as that of the Tutor, it is necessary that the teacher becomes aware, through feedback, of how well he or she has supported the student's learning experience and equally, how well he or she has the student's understanding at the knowledge level.

Apart from the kind of feedback each teacher can receive during the team meetings, feedback for teachers can take various other forms, including, for instance:

a   *direct/immediate feedback for teachers from the student*, which happens during each curriculum time slot. Direct feedback is initiated by the teacher who seeks the student's immediate reaction to the teacher's advice, guidance, instruction, analysis or demonstration. The teacher might ask how the student feels about the session, whether they have any further questions, which part of the session is not yet clear to them, and so forth. Such direct feedback for the teacher helps to improve his or her teaching and hence, the support that the student needs. Similarly, teachers can collect samples of students' work on a particular topic or an individual project to understand how students individually and as a group have learned the content or grasped a set of desirable skills;

b   *termly feedback for teachers from the student* through a questionnaire that each student can complete anonymously. The questionnaire includes both scaled feedback showing to what extent the student has appreciated a teacher's work, together with anecdotal feedback in the form of narrative which invites the student to give details of what they see as the teacher's strengths and the aspects of his or her teaching that could be strengthened. As the questionnaires are completed anonymously, the potential power imbalance between the student and the teacher is reduced to the minimum and the student can be more open in providing the constructive and frank feedback that the teacher needs;

c   *feedback for the teacher from the student portfolio,* which contains the oeuvre of the students over an academic year. This provides feedback for the teacher in terms of how well the student has progressed both in the particular area in which the teacher has supported the student, and in their holistic development. In particular, in students' reflective learning journals, which are part of the students' portfolios and in which the students document their experiences, the teachers can draw some feedback on how his or her support has enabled the students to achieve the goals they have set for themselves;

d   *feedback for the teacher from peers,* especially from the Mentors on the students' progress with a particular aspect of their learning, for example cognitive development or project work, as well as feedback from peer observation and team teaching. Feedback from peers requires a safe space and trust. We will return to this in Chapter 8 when we discuss school governance and how to create a culture of collaboration and co-creation;

e   *feedback for the teacher from school leadership,* which takes the form of regular review of teachers' work overtime, their ongoing professional development, regular reflection on practice and termly training programmes. Feedback from the leadership focuses on teachers' holistic development, including their commitment and motivation; again, we will expand on this in Chapter 8.

In this section, we introduce the notion of learning feedback which contains two components: (1) feedback directed at supporting the students' learning, improvement and overall development, including the feedback for students explained in Table 5.1; and (2) evaluative feedback of the processes that help shape the students' learning experiences. This mainly involves standing back and valuing what the teachers have been doing and exploring ways that the teachers could further improve their practices, and largely refers to the feedback for teachers explained in Table 5.2.

Learning review

Given the human-centred principles and values described in this handbook, a human-centred model for learning review should

• be respectful of the individual by allowing young people to present their progress in ways that they see fit, although with guided self-reflection;
• document progress in ways which are meaningful for students;

Table 5.1 Four levels of feedback for the student

Feedback for students	Purpose	Frequency	From whom	Type
Qualities of project/task	Practical advice on the strengths of project/task, and suggestions for improvement	Ongoing	Project Supervisor Tutors	Informal/verbal formal/written
Learning processes	An overview of the student's learning journey over a period of time to enhance her approach to learning	Half-termly	Project Supervisor Tutors	Formal
Learning dispositions	Feedback on the student's commitment, responsibility and motivation	Ongoing / termly	Mentor	Informal/formal
Overall development	Practical advice on the student's overall development	Ongoing / termly	Mentor	Informal/formal

Table 5.2 Different forms of feedback for teachers

Feedback for teachers	Purpose	Frequency	From whom	Type
Direct feedback	Helps to improve students' learning experiences during teaching sessions	Ongoing	Students	Informal/verbal
Termly feedback	Identifies the teacher's strengths from a student's perspective and aspects of teaching that can be strengthened	Termly	Students	Formal/ questionnaire
Feedback through students' work	Shows how well the teacher has supported the student in achieving their own goals	Annually	Students	Informal
Peer feedback	Identifies teacher's strengths from peers' perspectives and aspects of teaching that can be strengthened	Ongoing	Other teachers	Informal/formal
Feedback from school leaders	Provides feedback on teachers' holistic development	Half-termly	School leaders	Formal

- include ways of showing that the human-centred aims of the school are being met, for example that students are developing qualities on an emotional level, that is, that the school is educating the person as a whole;
- offer helpful feedback to students without dictating the learning processes;
- be integrated into the school curriculum in meaningful ways, rather than as an add-on.

In a human-centred school, learning review must be located within the curriculum structure as proposed in Chapter 3, which facilitates students' progress in five broad areas:

1　developing the qualities that enable a person to engage appropriately with the valuable activities of a human life;
2　gaining a sense of who they are and where they are going in their life's trajectories;
3　developing the emotional maturity and sensitivities to engage in relationships;
4　gaining the motivation, confidence and cognitive abilities to understand things for oneself and in relation to others and the world;
5　gaining knowledge, concepts and skills specific to certain subject areas, including general knowledge.

One way to review the progress that each student is making in relation to these five areas, could be through the following practical ideas.[2]

Qualities

The aim here is to develop the qualities that enable a person to engage appropriately with the valuable activities of a human life. For this purpose, students might write an annual *qualities review*, which is an extended reflection that documents and explores the qualities that they have focused on developing that year. The review could be in the form of a formal written paper or an informal reflective journal that is based on the student's ongoing reflection in Direction Time and provides an opportunity for them to draw a coherent picture of their activities in relation to the qualities they have been nurturing, together with the general learning goals developed with their Mentor. This review could be included in the student's portfolio to demonstrate their learning journey.

Direction

The focus for the students here is to gain a sense of who they are and where they are going. Students write a paper answering the questions 'Who Am I? What Could I Be?' to explore their understanding of their past and present and how this informs their future projections. This paper should be a reflection of students' current orientation to themselves, drawing on what they have learned in Direction Time. Once again, this paper could be included in the portfolio, together with the general learning goals developed with the Mentor.

Relationships

Here, the emphasis is on developing the emotional maturity and sensitivity to engage in more meaningful relationships. Students select one session of Group Time that they found to be an especially significant learning experience and build a reflective or creative project around it. This may explore other experiences in and outside of Group Time as part of contextualising and discussing the issues raised. This reflective project may be supported by the Facilitator (e.g. in the final session of Group Time). In addition to being a self-evaluative process, such creation should itself be a learning process.

Cognitive capacities

This means gaining the motivation, confidence and cognitive abilities to understand things for oneself. One might collect a selection of independent projects on which the student has worked over the past year. These projects should already include a log recording all key decisions in the process of research. Students might write a brief reflection on the projects' values in their lives.

Knowledge and skills

This centres on gaining knowledge, concepts and skills specific to certain subject areas, including general knowledge, and is divided into three key areas. Every half term, for each class (of Subject Time, General Knowledge Time and Cognitive Development Time), the following could take place:

1   Prior to beginning any module or course, a student creates a Learning Agreement with their Mentor, which includes personalised aims specific to the course or module. At the end of the term, the student reviews the Learning Agreement with their Tutor and/or Mentor. The young person is asked to assess how they have done in relation to those aims. One could annex to these personalised documents general descriptions of the aims and content of the course.
2   Students prepare an indicative portfolio of submissions and classwork. Work is selected by students based on what they are most proud of and what is most representative of the quality of their work. This encourages students to reflect critically on the values of their work and to appreciate the effort they have put in and the journey they have taken in order to bring these pieces of work forward. Students might also write a short commentary, as part of the portfolio, which reflects on the aims of the course and self-evaluates their progress in relation to these aims.
3   Mentors and/or Tutors write a qualitative report on each student's progress (without grades, of course). The narrative for such a report will be personalised reflecting the principles listed above and will be caring in tone and directive in flagging areas in which a student needs to make progress, as well as how they might achieve this.

In summary, in the above model students could provide the following:

1   three extended reflective papers/projects per year. These papers draw heavily on the ongoing self-reflection and documentation taking place throughout the year, for example in the Learning Agreements;
2   short reflective documents both in general and on each course/module throughout the year, which include the relevant Learning Agreements;
3   a selection of work for each course, each term, presented in a portfolio.

These written reflections and reflective documents will be shared with Tutors, Coaches, Facilitators and Mentors. The following are merits of such a model.

a   Preparation of the materials should form powerful educational experiences in their own right. Young people learn to reflect on the educational aims of the term and on their own growth, in ways that respect their autonomy.
b   Students are active participants and agents in the learning feedback process – all reflection on their progress is dialogic, including the written reflective accounts.

c   There is no assessment of the student. Instead, the process teaches students to critically evaluate their work in relation to academic standards with the guidance of
Mentors and Tutors.

There may be more creative ways to exhibit and evaluate the qualities of the student's
work, such as the example given in Box 5.1.

Box 5.1 TeachHUB suggestions of alternative evaluative tasks

TeachHUB suggests 40 alternative evaluative tasks, including ideas such as:

- writing a song about a topic;
- creating a scrapbook page;
- designing a museum exhibit;
- creating a trivia game;
- writing an advice column for someone with a science problem;
- fictionalised diary entries;
- creating a documentary (e.g. film or radio) on a topic;
- writing a eulogy for an overused word in a student assignment;
- creating an internet resource list about a topic.

(http://www.teachhub.com/40-alternative-assessments-learning)

Because the process of developing these learning reviews is highly reflective, students
are unlikely to feel that this model is onerous and disconnected from their learning. In
this way, this method should enhance learning rather than instrumentalising it. This
way of documenting and reviewing students' progress is grounded in the conviction
that to understand a student's learning and experience of schooling, we must listen to
them. By bringing together self-reflective projects and self-selected portfolios, the model
allows young people to present their learning progress in their own ways. It gives them
their own voice and locates their voice in a dialogue with teachers and peers.

Portfolios

In this chapter, we have explored some alternatives to testing and grades that can be
applied in some schools. These help review the students' learning experiences as a
whole, provide ongoing feedback for their holistic development and equally, offer the
opportunity for teachers to review students' work and how well their learning and
experiences have been supported. Such an alternative should not be called 'assessment'
because it is fundamentally non-judgemental.

In this section, we use a practical case study of a portfolio to illustrate how these
human-centred alternatives can be implemented within schools. A portfolio, as we
shall see, contains non-judgemental self-evaluative writing, narrative feedback from
teachers, records of peer feedback, visual records, written papers, documentation and
other co-created and innovative ideas. The following are for illustrative purposes only,
and are here to encourage imaginative and creative ideas from teachers and students.

Student portfolios contain a selection of the students' work, which is intended to represent their progress over time. A *learning portfolio* is a record of the students' educational journeys and their progress over a period of time. Such a portfolio includes a systematic collection of students' narratives, reflective journals, learning plans and project work. It contains significant evidence of the young person's learning, such as the following:

i   Learning Agreement;

ii   research questions for project work, research plan, methodology and written report;

iii complete hands-on projects, outline of development and report;

iv a list of books, literature and other information read over time, and reviews written about materials read;

v   learning journals which document and record significant learning experiences and memorable moments over time, reflecting on questions such as 'What have I enjoyed in doing the project', 'How have I become more daring or more confident', 'Who has helped me most', and so forth;

vi tasks completed as part of any formal training or cognitive development programmes (e.g. mathematics topics, reading skills, etc.);

vii personal statement at present (e.g. interests and hobbies, personal strengths and characteristics, values and worldviews, dreams and ideal work or occupation as an adult, etc.);

viii personal narratives, website, social networking sites, résumé, and other autobiographical information, and so forth.

Portfolios serve only the learning needs of the student (and the derivative feedback needs of the teachers). They are internal to the learning process. This means that it is important that when a learning portfolio is constructed, the content is selected and assembled by the student in consultation and dialogue with the Mentor. This is strategically important because through dialogue the student can better understand the relevant criteria necessary to demonstrate their learning.

Because the portfolio aims to provide a story about the students' learning journeys over time, it is necessary to reflect on their progress and achievements as well as aspects or areas that require further progress or are of concern. In doing so, students can set their own learning goals and understand the relevance of the programme of studies to their personal development. When portfolios are well integrated with learning, they can also help students to understand their talents, strengths, weaknesses and needs, and to see their own progress and development over time. Only in these ways can portfolios truly serve the needs of students for learning feedback and offer the opportunity for self-reflection and evaluative review, which includes a deeper understanding of the learning process and the transformation in themselves.

Teachers can use the portfolio as a diagnostic tool either for the individual or the class as a whole; equally, the portfolios can offer feedback for the teachers with regard to their ongoing engagement with the student and become an integral part of the teachers' professional reflection.

However, teachers and students may both feel that portfolios are subjective as a form of learning review, especially when there is no yardstick by which to measure what one takes to be a good piece of work or a project of a reasonable standard. Therefore, it is the responsibility of the Mentor, the Tutors and Project Supervisors to ensure that the student has a good understanding of the relevant standards involved in particular projects or tasks, such as an essay, an art project or a dance choreography. In fact, reviewing these samples of work with the students can offer the opportunity for them to self-review or even peer review, which in turn provides a meaningful opportunity for them to internalise project standards or the qualities of a good piece of work. In this case, the teacher might give the students a checklist in terms of what would count as the strengths or positive qualities of a piece of work; sometimes, the teacher may even offer a spectrum of qualities that are sought in a project or a piece of work so that the students can gain an idea of the direction in which they are heading next.

We must mention here that implementing a portfolio as an alternative to testing and grades is not easy, but it can nevertheless be very effective. Portfolios show the cumulative efforts and learning of a particular student over time. They offer valuable data about student improvement and skill mastery. Along with student reflection, that data provides valuable information about how each student learns and what is important to him or her in the learning process.

Teachers can also obtain feedback from other teachers who could use the students' portfolios creatively. Inviting comments and feedback on the students' work from another teacher who is not familiar with these students' usual standards and qualities will give the teacher more accurate and more helpful feedback.

Another way of organising the portfolio is for the students to select, collect and create a snapshot that captures their own evaluation and appreciation of learning. This can serve both the teachers' need for feedback on the students' progress, and the students' understanding of their own improvement and learning. Giving students a choice of what is placed in their portfolios and trusting students to critically reflect on their own learning process and journeys also helps the students to feel that learning is fundamentally their own responsibility.

Box 5.2 Madeley Court School's Personal Record of School Experience

Madeley Court School has adopted a learning review procedure pioneered by the Sutton Centre in Nottingham, another progressive comprehensive school. The Personal Record of School Experience was used to replace the conventional school report. Believing that there should be continuing dialogue between teachers, parents and students and that the process of learning requires active and ongoing self-reflection and evaluation, each student at the age of 14 was encouraged to create a folder which contained regular comments by the student, teachers, parents and work experience employers, as well as feedback on their experiences in other activities, such as sports, music and community engagement. By the time a student had completed their secondary education, they had a complete, personalised school experience record.

(www.hse.org.uk)

Box 5.2 shows an example of a learning review procedure, captured on the Human-Scale Education website. It is based on the learning review and feedback approach adopted by Madeley Court School in Telford, Shropshire. The school was founded in 1977 with an ethos that was largely aimed at human transformation, akin to a human-centred vision. It was closed in 1983.

Although not an exact model of a portfolio as we have proposed, the Madeley Court School's Personal Record of School Experience was used to show future employers and further education institutions the learning processes and journey students had been through and the learning and understanding they had developed, as well as how their peers, teachers, parents and others around them had appreciated these experiences.

We could even take this idea a step further because some elements of the student's feedback needs can be integrated into the life of the community. One can imagine that different pathways might serve to satisfy the school's needs for feedback, review and evaluation. For example:

1 a daily meeting where the student meets with his or her Tutor to discuss experience of activities or project work, and to receive feedback from the Mentor and/or from peers;

2 a weekly review with the Mentor on a one-on-one basis. This is an occasion to discuss progress overtime, readjust goals and deal with the challenges experienced;

3 a bi-weekly student 'lecture' where young people take turns to give talks on topics that they have been investigating. This could be about developing a middle-game in chess, a presentation about the River Gambia, showing refraction through a prism, or an analysis of one of Bach's fugues. Student lectures give the opportunity for peers and teaching staff to see how well the young person is doing in his or her research work, and offer feedback on the topic;

4 a half-termly meeting with teachers (Mentor, Facilitator and Tutors) where parents are invited to discuss the young person's work progress, meeting their needs, and how all parties can work together to support the young person's learning;

5 a termly open day or evening organised by the young people to which parents, teachers, school administrators and other staff are invited. Students take turns to report on their learning and take the opportunity to showcase work, present projects and discuss their experiences of curriculum activities. At the end of the report, students could give performances or stage a talent show. This is an occasion to take stock, review the young person's learning experience and celebrate progress;

6 a termly exhibition co-organised by the teaching staff and the students. Each student presents their learning portfolios to peers, teachers and families. School administrators, governors, trustees and other members in the wider community will be invited to this occasion. The student is expected to explain how they have identified the questions and worked through the projects, and the audience provides feedback, shows appreciation and holds engaging conversations with the young people;

7 a yearly student conference organised by the staff where the participants (students and adults from within and without the school) come together to explore a theme of common interest in depth. This is an occasion to write and present papers, organise debates or share individual research on the topic.

With proposals like these, we can see that the community can have some sense of how the students are doing, through events that bring together the community without the need for grades and exams.

In Chapter 9, we will provide more illustrative examples of the constructive use of the portfolio, including myriad possibilities of evaluative learning portfolios brought by digital technologies, as well as other alternative approaches to learning feedback and review.

Conclusion

The different learning review and evaluation models introduced in this chapter are designed to meet the learning feedback needs of students. The portfolios produced are part of and expressions of an integrated personal learning experience. As such, they should have no application beyond the school itself.

As we stressed at the beginning, a human-centred approach rejects the idea that there should be a catch-all category of assessment that satisfies the needs of all stakeholders. Potential future employers and further educational institutions have informational needs that are different from the external accountability needs of government and these are quite different from the learning needs of students, which we take as paramount.

However, a full human-centred approach involves systemic changes. Such changes will require a complete separation of the five aims of educative evaluation mentioned at the beginning of this chapter. We believe that it is entirely possible to satisfy the informational needs of employers, higher educational institutions, governments and the public without instrumentalising and compromising learning as testing tends to do.

Schools have to operate within the existing system based on examinations and grades and students must sit public exams. Therefore, the important question is to what extent a school can focus the learning processes of the young people on their integral development, rather than on the exams. On the one hand, training that is focused directly on public exams might help students to do better in terms of grades, but this would not transform the lives of the students. On the other hand, students who are confident and motivated and who have strong cognitive skills pertaining to thinking and reading will tend to do well in public exams.

The onus is on the school to mitigate the harm that the current system causes by focusing the school around a different set of values. It is vital that the discourse of the school retains its human-centred ethos *despite* the external expectations, and that the exams should not be allowed to dictate the focus of the classroom.

Notes

1 As we shall see in Chapter 8, a human-centred approach to teachers' professional development is not through teachers' performance management. Instead, it is carried out through regular review/reflection on practice. Currently, performance management is connected to assessing the teachers' abilities to teach to the national curriculum content, which is linked to the students' attainments during high-stakes exams. By contrast, a human-centred approach to teaching review is focused on the holistic development of the teacher.

2 What we propose below should be understood as suggestions, which are open to interpretation and review as a school sees fit.

Chapter 6

Becoming a human-centred educator

Overview

In this chapter, we will explain how schools might support teachers in their work and nurture their personal and professional growth. This support and nurturing has two objectives: first, that educational processes in the school enable the holistic development of the students, and second, that teachers themselves can appreciate or connect to the value of teaching and flourish through their work. The chapter is structured as follows:

- getting to know human-centred values;
- human-centred education in the classroom;
- team meetings, regular training and individual personal review;
- appreciative inquiry;
- other kinds of teacher support;
- understanding adolescence.

From the point of view of a functioning human-centred school, 'Team meetings, regular training and individual personal review' and 'Understanding adolescence' define the kinds of minimal teacher support that needs to be in place. 'Appreciative inquiry' defines their methodology. The section 'Other kinds of teacher support' defines some additional options. The sections 'Getting to know human-centred values' and 'Human-centred education in the classroom' characterise some of the processes needed to become a functioning human-centred school.

This handbook offers an account of the meaning of HCE. We have suggested a variety of practices to show ways in which HCE might be implemented in schools.

However, a school does not automatically become a learning community merely by having a human-centred vision and an ethos of care. The ethos will need to be built and rebuilt, and the vision and principles revisited with the staff, students, parents and members of the community. A human-centred school is a communal project of constructing a living culture. Thus, within the school there will be processes that facilitate relationships and listening, participation and responsibility, collaboration and co-action. The role of the teachers is central to these processes.

Once the community has made a commitment towards a shared vision, one of the next steps will be to establish some 'institutional architecture' as recommended in Chapter 2. Within this architecture, the training and support for teachers and their professional development are paramount. This ongoing process demands leadership commitment. Teaching is a vocation, and the building of teaching capabilities requires stimulation and inspiration. The process enables teachers to enrich their teaching experience rather than merely conforming to performance expectations.

What are the main elements with regard to teachers' development? First is the teachers' initiation into human-centred values and principles. This may require two processes: (a) a preparatory reflection on their personal convictions regarding educational aims and (b) an outward examination of the meaning of HCE.

The second element is that teachers put human-centred educational values into practice in their teaching. We discussed this theme in Chapter 4. The process whereby a school moves towards a more human-centred curriculum will take time. Presumably, in most schools it will initially involve adding components to the traditional curriculum such as mentoring, cognitive and sharing sessions. This means that most of the teachers will still be teaching subjects in large classrooms. However, these teachers will want to begin the process of adapting their pedagogy to the human-centred approach. This suggests the following question: In the absence of a committed HCE institution, how can teachers put human-centred values and principles into practice? We answer this question in the section 'Human-centred education in the classroom'.

The third element comes more into play as the school phases out of the transitional period. As part of its institutional architecture, the HCE school will arrange regular sessions for teachers to support each other and to share good teaching practices. It will also organise periodic training and review sessions. We discuss this in the section 'Team meetings, regular training and individual personal review'.

The fourth element is the importance of staff understanding well the needs and challenges confronting adolescents. The school might consider providing training to develop such awareness (see 'Understanding adolescence').

In this chapter, we visit each of these elements and describe how schools can nurture teachers' personal and professional growth so that the school is focused on the holistic development of each person, students and staff alike.

Getting to know human-centred values

We propose two processes to help introduce teachers to HCE values.

The first provides opportunities for teachers to reflect on their personal convictions about educational aims and values, as well as theories of learning. One way to do this is for teachers to work in small groups and share personal learning biographies.[1] This method is being employed increasingly in teacher training programmes worldwide. It involves teachers sharing narratives about their lives as learners. In reflecting on their lives as learners, teachers often find connections between their own experiences and theories of learning. When reflecting on the meaning of these experiences, teachers can realise the whole-person nature of engagement. These biographical projects could shed light on the past sources of their current commitment to teaching, and this process renews that commitment.

Let us outline how a learning biography could become part of a teacher's professional development process. Participants could

1   attend an introductory seminar to prepare them for deep reflection, help them understand the methodology of sharing learning biographies and to explore key

concepts involved in biographical learning. During this seminar, the group would engage in dialogue about self-inquiry through life history and memories, learning theories, personal identity and other connected concepts;

2   prepare and reflect on one's life history with a focus on key experiences, activities, events and significant others in one's life. This could be done during holiday time or in personal time. The purpose of the reflection is to consider questions such as 'What are the key events and transitions in my life?' and 'In what ways have these shaped the person I am now and who I am to become in the future?' The core of reflection can be any experiences of learning, from childhood to present, from formal learning through schooling or other educational institutions, to informal, incidental and accidental learning;

3   share oral narratives of individual journeys in learning with the group. This is often a most creative and engaging session. Participants could use diverse media to show their journeys: posters, slideshow of photos, drawings, music and songs, objects and memorabilia;

4   after the initial sharing, provide and receive feedback from peers, highlighting the connections between lived experiences and learning. Further group dialogue will help consolidate shared understanding (and theorisation) of learning, and explore ways to integrate the new understanding in one's ongoing teaching and learning practices as well as one's ways of being.

It might be a good idea to begin the academic year with the learning biography. This is because such reflection process could help stronger relationships. The more deeply teachers share personal narratives with one another, the stronger the bond between them. In addition, because such sharing is in itself a whole-person learning experience, teachers could take the opportunity to internalise the meaning of HCE.

The second kind of process we recommend consists in seminars and discussions about the meaning of HCE. Regular seminars on the aims of education would give teachers the opportunity to connect these with human-centred practices. These seminars could be led by senior members of the staff team or educators from outside the school, and their main purpose would be to introduce teachers to HCE by stimulating reflection about the aims and values of education. These sessions are introductory but they could become ongoing and, as such, they would become part of teacher training support, which we will discuss in the 'Team meetings' section below.

Human-centred education in the classroom

How do we, as teachers, put human-centred values into practice? This question may seem especially baffling for traditional teachers. As a subject teacher in a state school, one is faced with large classes of students, some of whom are disengaged or disaffected and one is under the pressure of a national curriculum and public exams. Where are the spaces to construct personalised curriculum for each individual student?

The answer isn't that complicated. Once teachers have caught the main ideas of HCE, and once they have seen teaching from this fresh perspective, then they will naturally have a host of questions about their own practices such as 'How can I do this differently?' and 'What should I do about this and that?' What we are trying to show in this handbook is that there are no set answers like a ready-made recipe. The only suggestions are those that define the relevant processes that need to take place. In other words, a handbook like this provides guidance for setting up processes without predetermining what the outcomes of those processes will be. Teaching is an extraordinarily fine and complex art. As teachers, we need to share good practices.

In Chapter 2, we distinguished three levels of putting HCE into practice: the systemic, the institutional and the individual. First, this handbook proposes HCE as a new vision of the educational system as a whole. In other words, HCE is a system-wide vision for education. Second, however, in this handbook we only present HCE at the institutional level, as a possible ideal for schools. Institutions can become more human-centred, even when the system is not. Third, in a similar vein, individual teachers can become more human-centred even when the institution in which they work isn't. At this individual level, without institutional change, the individual teacher will face many difficulties and, therefore, it is not surprising that becoming human-centred may feel like an up-hill task. Nevertheless, there are things that can be done at the individual level to make education more human-centred. In this spirit, here are six general comments that might help.

First, in our experience, when teachers are asked about teaching that has touched their students deeply, most respond with stories that depend on their showing individual care for a student. Lives are usually transformed by individual attention. For instance, if a student looks bored or switched off in the classroom, it often transforms the situation if the teacher asks to see the student after class and then expresses concern: 'I noticed that you looked distracted in class. Is everything okay? Do you need something?' Such simple questions invite the student to express their problems and if one follows this process through, one may see the young person transform. These meetings can be brief but the follow-up is very important.

Notice how the approach advocated here makes some important implicit presuppositions. It implies the unspoken assumption that unruly, distracted and unmotivated attitudes don't belong in the classroom. It implies this is because any student who displays such attitudes will be challenged, albeit gently and lovingly, to explain why. Yet, the assumption remains unspoken and implicit and, as such, it is much more powerful than any explicit command that might be disobeyed. Implicit expectations define a culture. Explicit assumptions are relegated to commands.

The second presupposition is that a student who displays attitudes of being disengaged and so on isn't behaving in a way that deserves punishment. It is rather that such a student needs special care and attention. This is a subtle but important point: the assumption is that such negative attitudes are not acceptable, but there is absolutely no moralistic or judgemental tone to that assumption. The human-centred approach generally does not take unruly behaviour as immoral, as behaviour worthy of condemnation and punishment. Instead, the human-centred approach tends to take such behaviour as an expression of a malaise or problem that needs resolution or attentive care.

The human-centred approach looks proactively for opportunities to help students develop holistically. The student doesn't need to be overtly disaffected in order for him or her to benefit from care. For example, a student who is mentally active but who doesn't write well might benefit greatly from a few moments of guidance about his or her writing. A very bright student might need extra challenges. A student who is trying especially hard might need encouragement and recognition. Here is another example: as several authors have pointed, it is good to notice the students who try to be invisible in class. Again, there is usually a reason for their being this way, and once it comes out, this starts a process through which their situation may eventually be transformed.

The second general comment concerns classroom atmosphere. It is very difficult to work creatively in a classroom in which the atmosphere is antipathetic. The ambience doesn't have to be hostile for this issue to be a concern. It only needs a few apathetic individuals to create a classroom mood of stony indifference. With a large class and a few disengaged students, the feeling of drudgery in a class might be palpable. When the mood of the class is glum or disenchanted, a teacher may feel overwhelmed. Sometimes, there seems to be no option but to wade into a classroom and carry on with a pre-planned lesson in spite of the class's indifference.

The human-centred approach will advocate the idea that there are always alternatives to wading in. In other words, there are ways to lift the mood of the group so that the lesson plan doesn't become a chore. The classroom feeling of student apathy doesn't count as a reason to instrumentalise the educational process. Even if the students are apathetic, there are ways to lift the group without selling out to traditional instrumentalisation.

The primary way to transform the atmosphere of a disengaged classroom is to identify the persons who are most effectual in creating this classroom culture. Short one-on-one meetings with these persons will eventually change their effect on the rest of the room. Another way to transform the atmosphere is try out different interactions and tones with the class as a whole in the initial few minutes. The interactions that occur before the group plunges into the material can define the mood and motivation of everyone in the class. These tone-setting moments are vital.

The third general comment is the huge importance of cognitive contextualisation, as we mentioned earlier. For instance, if a lesson is not properly contextualised, then the students will not understand why and what they are learning. HCE provides the broad contextualisation of education, as we saw in Chapter 1: individual development.

Contextualisation can also comprise meta-lessons. In a meta-lesson, one isn't teaching the course material; one makes important observations about the material or the way that one is teaching it: 'Please think about this in the following way because . . .'. Even in a very knowledge-based class, there are meta-lessons that the teacher needs to convey. For example, why do we think about this mathematical problem in this way? What do we learn about being a mathematician from this? Why is this important? In any knowledge-based class, there are a host of meta-lessons that the student needs to understand in order to contextualise better the knowledge being taught. For example, we draw attention to the way an experiment is set up or designed and in so doing, highlight certain scientific virtues. The point is that meta-learning needs to be distinguished as something apart and as something to which the students need to attend. How do we do this in a class? Some teachers change their tone of voice; some change their physical position. In general, in comparison with subject-led teaching, these meta-lessons often need strengthening. They provide the kind of cognitive and motivational contextualisation that students need. They provide the bridge to more complete human-centred approaches. For example, the links to virtues or qualities can be provided through such contextualising.

Fourth, a teacher is a role model, and in a human-centred school teachers embody core human values such as care and questioning as part of their way of being. While young people can be impressionable, at the same time they can be highly perceptive and not easily persuaded by teachers who are not convinced of what they practise at the school. Authentic teachers are more capable of connecting with young people.

Teachers need a lot of support to become effective role models. This indicates that teachers' inner sense of who they are needs to be integrated with what they value and how they teach. It implies that teachers are committed to the values inherent in teaching as something more than a job and a role. Therefore, teacher training becomes more than professional development. It requires opportunities for teachers themselves to develop as persons. Even if a school already has a values-based culture, such an ethos cannot be imposed on any individual teacher. Even if a school has a strong leadership that embodies human-centred values, this doesn't mean that all teachers will automatically pick up that ethos in a ripple effect. Teachers will need the opportunity to work through these issues for themselves.

Fifth, one of the big struggles for teachers is how to find the time to work individually with students. The day is packed. Therefore, the advice given earlier may seem impractical: there isn't time to implement it. In contrast to this, many of the teachers that we have spoken to in our research acknowledge that their day is often taken up with busy-busy work. For example, some teachers feel obliged to teach material that has little long-term impact on their students. Others feel frustrated with administrative tasks that are time-consuming but have little utility.

If correct, this is a conflict upon which to reflect. On the one hand, as teachers, we recognise the huge importance of more personalised attention for students. It can change many fundamentals, if only we had the time. On the other hand, we recognise that many of the activities that absorb this time are not productive. The system forces us to spend time engaged in teaching and administrative activities that are not transformative.

Of course, it is part of life that time tends to be spent on activities of less priority. In this regard, the solution to the conflict lies in the specific context of the individual and the school. There are always ways to be less hounded by busy-busy work so that one can be more free to express care in tangible ways. In conclusion, the teacher who is committed to HCE values needs to find more time in which to dedicate individual attention to students. How this is done depends on the specific context of the school.

The sixth general comment: find allies and spaces to share with colleagues. It is difficult to implement HCE in an educational system that isn't human-centred, and even harder in a school that isn't. Nevertheless, teachers who want to make their teaching more human-centred can collaborate and support each other. For instance, when teachers in a school share that they spend a lot of time on activities of less value and that they would prefer to have more time to dedicate to individual students, the effect can be liberating. They can begin to swap ideas about how to change this frustrating situation.

In a school that is becoming human-centred, teachers will have the opportunity for this kind of sharing on a regular basis. For that to happen, the school management will need to block out regular time slots for teacher mutual support sessions. As we shall see below, teachers might organise workshops amongst themselves that are dedicated to exploring specific challenges within the current student cohort. In these workshops, a teacher or a team of teachers may wish to share concerns and invite other teachers to help them explore the best possible pedagogical approaches to support their own learning or the learning of their students. These sharing sessions are important for other reasons. There are many aspects to the art of teaching in a human-centred way that can be shared.

Team meetings, regular training and individual personal review

For a school to embody human-centred values there needs to be meaningful support for the teachers' personal growth, which includes but goes beyond professional development. For this reason, we suggest that the school runs three kinds of sessions.

Team meetings

On specific days (e.g. Wednesday afternoons), when students are engaged in sports or creative activities, the staff team can take the time for open-ended conversation or meetings focused on the learning journeys and needs of individual students. Such team meetings are much needed to coordinate the teachers' work and for engaging in critical constructive reflection on one's own and others' practices. They are a space for sharing and mutual support.

These meetings would be in addition to the regular training sessions, which would follow a pre-established structure with more clearly defined objectives. The team meeting sessions could be open-ended, and from time to time focus on specific emerging concerns. Such meetings serve several purposes.

First, meetings are necessary for collective planning. The human-centred curriculum provides only a framework that holds the different pedagogical strategies together (what we call 'the ingredients for map making'). Because of this, the actual content of the curriculum activities are emergent and require planning.

Second, whole-team planning ensures that all educational practices, such as curriculum design, pedagogical strategies and learning reviews, work concertedly towards supporting the student's whole-person development.

Third, meetings help ensure that the objectives are owned by all members of staff and this ownership helps motivate the teachers to work towards common goals.

Finally, meetings create a space for teachers to be involved in evaluative reflection: 'What are students' experiences during this term?', 'How well have the students progressed over the last year?', 'What are the areas of knowledge that need strengthening?', 'How might we guide students better in their project work?' Such team evaluation is another safe space, complemented by teachers' own professional development. Like their professional development sessions, such evaluative processes are not judgemental about teachers' work. Instead, the evaluation centres on reviewing the qualities of the students' learning and development.

These sessions provide a safe and confidential space for teachers to support each other. The content of these sessions would be decided by the teachers, with some guidance from the leadership team. They would certainly include the sharing of teaching practices as discussed briefly in the previous section. The tone of these support sessions is very important. The kind of intimacy and honesty required precludes the participants being judgemental and defensive.

Regular training

Teachers will take part in regular training sessions to continue to learn how to teach in a more human-centred way. In this ongoing professional dialogue, the team leader (in a larger school) or the head teacher (in the case of a small school) and the teachers systematically explore ways to improve their teaching. These would include sessions on teachers' personal and professional development.

A primary concern for teaching staff is building trusting relationships with each other. This means that time will be allocated to enable the teachers to know each other well, including the strengths and gifts that everyone brings to the school. Earlier, we recommended a biographical approach to developing staff relationships and such an approach could easily be integrated into teacher training sessions. Box 6.1 offers an example.

Box 6.1 Building human relationships through teachers' life-story sharing

Aim: (a) To share life stories regarding one's choice to work in education; (b) to develop trust amongst the staff.

Timescale: Half day.

Setting: Informal and relaxed.

Step 1:   Exercises to make the space safe and bring the participants closer.

Step 2:   Briefing on the rationale and outlining the procedure, stressing deep listening and active engagement as well as confidence in stories.

Step 3:   Dividing participants into groups of five, maximising group diversity.

Step 4:   Individuals taking turns to share personal narratives; others attending to each story with respect and receiving the stories with appreciation.

Step 5:   Returning to the plenary in a large circle for open-ended conversations about how one's motivation affects the way one is engaged in personal and professional learning journeys. The discussion can be expanded to how one's commitment to education might impact one's experience as a teacher.

Step 6:   Wrapping up and concluding.

In addition to strengthening relationships, these training sessions can be topic-based, focusing on specific challenges that teachers are wrestling with, such as questions like 'How do we balance the different elements of the curriculum as a team?' or 'How do we ensure that students pay sufficient attention to the formative feedback?' This topic-based approach breaks with the traditional teacher training pattern, which often consists in being instructed with new teaching methods in workshops. Instead, topic-based training is rooted in the teachers' day-to-day practices; it meets the teachers' immediate needs and is supportive of their ongoing practices. Timely facilitation of topic-based training sessions can help reduce teachers' stress.

Another kind of training can be organised for a specific group of teachers, such as the Mentors or the Facilitators. The advantage of training the teachers in homogeneous groups is that it enables the focus of the conversation to be grounded in similar concerns such as 'How do we help students become engaged and motivated?' or 'What is the best way to develop project ideas with the student?' Training for each specific group provides the space to discuss each question in depth. Equally, it allows the teachers to empathise with each other, reflecting on the challenges of common practices and seeking mutual support.

Individual personal review

In a one-on-one confidential meeting, a person from the leadership team could discuss with teachers their concerns and progress. This is an opportunity for the school to show that it supports the teachers and that it wants them to progress.

In a human-centred school, the leadership team is concerned with the well-being of the teachers as colleagues and friends. They have and show a caring attitude towards the teachers and this is reflected in the way that the three kinds of sessions are run and set up. For instance, in the personal review sessions, the leadership team will regard the teacher as a whole person by placing their teaching practice within the context of their life history and their personal and professional aspirations.

All three kinds of sessions will integrate listening with dialogue. Compassionate listening is crucial in creating a safe space in which teachers can feel that they can be themselves and that they can become reflectively critical about their work.

Appreciative inquiry

It is important to adopt appropriate lenses through which to evaluate teaching practices. We suggest that these lenses be based on appreciation and inquiry rather than on being judgemental. This means that, for instance, reviewing with teachers their practices and reflecting on their development will focus on their strengths, qualities and potential, and will support them in taking risks to further develop their practices. One such approach proposed in Chapter 2 was *appreciative inquiry*, which can help to consolidate an understanding of the values within a school.

Teachers might work in teams and adopt the five-step process below, focusing their inquiry on shared educational values and good practices that aim at the best possible education for all:

1 *'Define' phase* – choosing the topic for the inquiry and determining how it will be undertaken.
2 *'Discover' phase* – discovering the best of what is through storytelling-based interviews.
3 *'Dream' phase* – dreaming of what might be.
4 *'Design' phase* – designing what should be in an ideal future.
5 *'Deliver' phase* – sustaining and underpinning the changes undertaken.

The cycle can be repeated, or where appropriate only part of the cycle may apply. What is good about this well-tested process is that it helps everyone engaged not only to own any change or new understanding, but also to proactively live by such an understanding or sustain the changes.

Box 6.2 An example of teachers' appreciative inquiry

All the staff members at the Swan Centre were invited to reflect and share thoughts on the following questions:

1   Describe a time that captures the Swan Centre working at its best as a learning community. What are the key ingredients/factors/features that make the Swan Centre such a learning community?
2   Without being modest, please share what you most value about yourself in terms of your contribution to this learning community.
3   Describe a time when you've felt most supported and/or integrated as part of the learning community. How does such an experience help you to better understand the meaning of a learning community?
4   What do you see as the core strengths of the Swan Centre team in cultivating a learning community? Why?
5   How would you like to see the learning community continue to grow and flourish?

Box 6.2 gives a clear example of how the appreciative approach can be integrated in teachers' reflections. When we first started the pilot project at the Swan Centre in the South East of England, which provides inclusive support to students with speech, language and communication needs or autistic spectrum conditions, we learned that the Centre itself already shared the HCE's aspiration of developing the school as a learning community. Therefore, as part of the teacher training, we launched an appreciative inquiry to find out the team's strengths in supporting a learning community and the areas in which the team would like to further explore and expand.

The group was divided into pairs and each pair shared their reflections on and insights into the questions in Box 6.2. Then the staff came together to discuss their emerging thoughts and thus, they built up a picture of where they had been going towards developing the Swan Centre into a learning community, the existing strengths and qualities that each individual had contributed, and how else they could work together to take the Centre's dream forwards.

The appreciative inquiry approach enabled the teachers to focus on their strengths rather than on their weaknesses and from that basis, the team could work towards what was possible rather than concentrate on the problems. This way of working creates a positive and virtuous circle of teachers' development and growth.

Other kinds of teacher support

So far, we have defined different kinds of meetings that would be held on a regular basis. A school might also consider other forms of support for teachers. In this section, we will examine mutual learning, enrichment, reflection and research, and space for tranquillity.

Mutual learning

We suggest that the school considers two types of mutual learning: team teaching, and peer mentoring or peer coaching. For the sake of simplicity, we will ignore the differences between peer mentoring and peer coaching.[2]

- Team teaching is practised in many schools and most teachers can recognise the merits of working in this way. It helps teachers to complement the strengths of one another, and it affirms the team's collective knowledge of the students, wisdom and talents. When teaching in a team, the teachers can learn from each other through mutual observation, appreciation, reflection and even critique. Once again as already pointed out, when the object of mutual learning is enhancing the students' learning experiences by way of teachers improving the way they teach, teachers can be more courageous and willing to embrace criticism and evaluative comments.
- Peer mentoring is a supporting and continued relationship between two individuals; often one is experienced and the other less so. The idea is that the senior colleague provides guidance, challenge and support to the younger colleague. Upon agreement between the peers, mentoring or coaching enables teachers to focus the conversations on very specific needs, both personal and professional. The peers do not have to be engaged in similar positions within the school, such as both being mentors or specialist tutors.

Mutual learning requires a safe environment where teachers are free from the fear of being judged, being compared with others or being undermined by colleagues. A human-centred school can engender the kind of safety and collegiality for mutual learning to thrive.

Enrichment

Teachers' enrichment occurs infrequently in schools, despite widespread recognition of its importance. It doesn't happen because teachers cannot be absent from classes in resource-stretched schools; for teachers to pursue enriching activities requires flexibility in the school's timetable. Fortunately, the human-centred school timetable does have such flexibility. The timetable contains project-based learning and peer-to-peer support. Furthermore, in a learning community there is a shared responsibility for learning and students will be more capable of studying independently without the need for monitoring or supervision because the motivation for learning comes from within.

Apart from creating spaces through flexible timetabling, the school can also liaise with other agencies to create such opportunities for teachers to attend enrichment activities. Such pathways may include:

- opportunities for higher learning;
- participating in conferences, workshops and seminars;
- visiting other schools;
- undertaking additional courses.

What counts as enrichment may be different for each individual teacher. This means that the school's leadership will plan the dialogues needed to identify the appropriate enrichment programmes for particular teachers as part of their individual personal reviews (see 'Individual personal review', above).

Teachers' reflection and research

Teachers' reflection and research into their own practices is another key to developing teaching and learning practices. Reflecting on one's educational values, beliefs, experiences and practices is central to being a teacher. Questioning and enquiring into one's work, experimenting with new ideas and collecting feedback are core aspects of teaching. Therefore, supporting teachers' reflection and research must form a crucial part of teacher training as it helps to frame teaching in such a way that theories, practices, epistemological values and aptitudes are integrated.

Formal training for teachers' reflection and research can involve introductory seminars and training workshops on how to become a reflective teacher researcher. Such training will focus on research paradigms and methodologies, and methods of reflection and inquiry. Schools could choose those methodologies that are practically implementable such as action research, case study, action learning and collaborative inquiry.

Schools could best support teachers' reflection and research by providing spaces for such activities throughout the academic year. This requires leaders to see the benefit of teacher's reflection and research and to trust teachers to use the time and space dedicated to such. Some teachers might use the time to pursue a master's programme in educational studies within a university; some teachers might use the space to document their own thoughts and observations from classes; others might use the opportunity to observe and enquire into other teachers' work. This culture of trust is one of the best approaches to encourage teachers to embark on research and inquiry.

Box 6.3 is an example of inquiry-based enrichment training with a group of Chinese secondary school teachers.

Box 6.3 Developing a relational way of learning: Chinese teachers' enrichment training

Aim:	(a) To explore how collaborative meaning making, co-inquiry and relationship building have impact on teachers' learning and understanding of relationships in the classroom; (b) create safe spaces for teachers and leaders to experience non-hierarchical relations and collegial connections.
Time scale:	One and a half days.
Setting:	Informal and relaxed.
Step 1:	Presenting key conceptual debates to illustrate multiple perspectives on the relevant topics and questions.
Step 2:	Using narrative self-inquiry to reflect on and understand the significance of relationships in their own learning lives.
Step 3:	Engaging in a variety of experiential and dialogic activities that aim at collaborative meaning making as a relational way of knowing.

Comment from teachers:

> We were drawn close to each other by this narrative experience and we
> became aware of the importance of relationships which were found both in
> the stories we shared and in the way the stories were shared and listened to.

A further possibility is that the school might establish a partnership with a university so that professional researchers are invited to collaborate with teachers in
reflection and research inquiry. The involvement of professional researchers can help
enhance teachers' research capability, enabling them to become more skilled at reflecting on their practice. The support of academic researchers can further enable teachers
to develop more systematic and rigorous approaches to reflection and inquiry.

Similar to other training priorities, supporting teachers' reflection and research
must ultimately be oriented towards the development and improvement of teachers'
practices, which have direct ramifications on young people's learning and well-being.

Spaces for tranquillity

Well-being training, mindfulness practices and emotional intelligence may support teachers in their personal and professional development. In many ways, teaching and supporting young people's development is intense work. Human-centred schools intentionally
create spaces for teachers to be quiet or have designated spaces so that teachers can have
solitary reflection or contemplative practices. These are what we call spaces for tranquillity.
Finding time and space in the school's busy timetable and teaching schedule to connect
with one's inner self, and inviting one's own 'heart and soul' to be present in teaching and
learning, is an important key to a teacher's whole-person development.

Understanding adolescence

Throughout this handbook, we highlight the importance of understanding adolescence
as a distinctive time in a human life.[3] Seminars about adolescence may help teachers build a more integrated and realistic view of young people's development. Such
training can enable teachers to acquire knowledge relating to adolescents' cognitive,
social, physical and emotional growth, as well as the influence of social and cultural
backgrounds. Such training can include up-to-date research on adolescence. The important point is that our common intuitions about adolescence may be misinformed. It is
another culture; it is an alien way of life that we, as teachers, need to learn about. These
seminars will help teachers to shape their practices within the different pedagogical
fields (i.e. in mentoring, group facilitation, subject teaching, and so forth).

The leadership team will identify the training themes so that they make a differ-
ence to the life of the community. We would suggest themes such as: learning theories; adolescents' cognitive, emotional and social development; exploring adolescents'
vulnerability and developmental opportunities; nurturing adolescent's responsibility;
facilitating collaborative learning; and building group dynamics.

Schools may invite experts in appropriate fields, such as psychologists, counsellors, youth workers, philosophers and others, to lead some of the training seminars and workshops. The seminars would combine sharing knowledge about adolescence with showcasing good and effective pedagogical strategies for working with students.

Conclusion

Teacher training aims at nurturing teachers' personal growth and professional development. In framing teacher training according to human-centred values, a school will foster a culture of care. A culture of care cannot be instilled piecemeal; nor can it be taught theoretically. It is constructed by the ways in which adults and young people relate to each other and work together. The more a school community and its members live and embody the values of care, the more such values become the fabric of the community.

Human-centred thinking defines leadership as collaborative rather than authoritarian. Collaborative processes of co-construction offer the opportunity for teachers to get to know each other better, resulting in closer relationships. Leadership becomes communal: leading is in part self-leading, and teacher training is mutual learning. Such a culture fosters teachers' commitment to their work and renews the school's values and good practices. Staff learning is not restricted to continuing professional development and learning more about one's subject area; it includes their holistic development of teachers as persons. We are not defined by our roles.

Notes

1 For instance, at the University of Sussex, the teachers doing the MA in Education Studies course tended to begin their research journey with writing a learning biography. See *Narrative Pedagogy* by Scherto Gill and Ivor Goodson, published by Peter Lang in 2011.

2 Peer coaching is defined as 'a confidential process through which two or more professional colleagues work together to reflect upon current practices; expand, refine and build new skills; share ideas; conduct action research; teach one another; or problem solve within the workplace' (Robbins, 1995, p. 206).

3 We see all phases of human development as distinct in terms of needs, challenges and opportunities. However, this is by no means to suggest that education must be age-dependent or that everyone has to grow and develop in a linear way.

Chapter 7

Educational governance

Overview

In this chapter, we will discuss how governance and its structures might shift in a human-centred learning community. This will involve a reconceptualisation of school governance. In particular, the notion of a learning community invites a shift from hierarchy towards participation and collaboration, from management towards engagement, and from strengthening institutional effectiveness towards cultivating humane relationships.

We will discuss educational governance through five major themes:[1]

- values and principles of governance;
- governance processes;
- governing bodies;
- collaboration and co-creation;
- accountability and responsibility.

The idea of a learning community challenges many of the assumptions of traditional governance. In particular, it stresses that learning and flourishing are the primary purposes of the community's coming together; these purposes change the nature of school governance.

Fundamentally, there are four important elements of human-centred governance:

First, the main aim of governance is to ensure that the educational processes, the teaching practices, the culture of the school and the environment each align well with the educational aims of the school. This is the most important purpose of governance, and it is achieved by embedding human values in the day-to-day living of the learning community. The activities of the community need to be consistent with its fundamental aims.

Second, it is essential that the vision for the school not be imposed from outside the community. Instead, it will belong to the community itself. Consequently, a key element of governance is to develop a culture of co-creation and collaboration. Such a culture can be cultivated in a number of ways, including the setting up of a governance structure that is conducive to collaborative work. Governance requires collaboration.

Under a human-centred vision, the development and flourishing of the community is the responsibility of all of its members, rather than just a small group of leaders. Thus, another element of school governance is the nurturing of the responsibility of all members of the community, including children, staff, parents and people within the local community. Governance requires nurturing.

Third, for this reason, a human-centred learning community requires respect for people's voices, including those of the students. This implies that governance will ensure that listening is an important aspect of the school's decision-making processes. From a human-centred perspective, traditional boundaries within schools are broken down, and instead, divergent spaces are created for developing trust, collaboration and critical reflection. Governance requires listening without barriers.

Fourth, this way of understanding governance does not undermine the importance of leadership, nor attempt to obscure accountability and transparency. The final element of human-centred governance is to ensure each of these elements is well connected with the others to form a coherent governance model. This is partly realised through developing clear policies and articulations of the school's practices. It is also partly accomplished by ongoing feedback, review and evaluation that do not instrumentalise the educational processes. In short, governance requires clear responsibilities.

In articulating how the different elements of governance work concertedly in guiding and supporting the learning community, this chapter offers some practical ideas that schools can adopt in order to begin a movement towards the much-desired systemic transformation in education and schooling.

Values and principles of governance

In human-centred education (HCE), the principles of governance are aligned with the overall HCE vision, as introduced in Chapter 1. For the purposes of governance, there are four fundamental values:

Wholeness: The first is the school's commitment to the holistic development of the young person. This holistic development will help enable the young person to feel at home in him or herself during adolescence, to live a life of well-being and dignity as an adult, to appreciate the value of harmonious relationships with others and to contribute to the betterment of society.

Community: The second value is the dedication to developing the school as a learning community. We can contrast a learning community with an institution. A community is more than an institution because its culture depends on the participation of its members. Thus, within a community good governance will ensure that the leadership team fosters human relationships at all levels. They will listen to and have dialogue with all members in their decision-making and in coordinating the actions of the community.

Respect: The third is respect for the young people, which implies that the school meets their diverse needs, which we described in Chapter 1. How does the school respect the students' current and future needs? It does so through the school environment, the curriculum, its pedagogy and learning feedback.

Responsibility: The fourth is a duty of care. This implies a non-invasive and holistic approach to evaluating the students' progress, the responsibilities of the staff and the school's educational accountability. HCE offers a counter-narrative to an education driven entirely by high-stakes testing. The same applies to performance management in general. Challenging the misconception of educational quality assurance (through high-stakes testing) requires propounding alternatives to exams and grades. The alternatives that we discussed in Chapter 5 are appropriate for a learning community as opposed to an institution. They provide accountability in terms of the quality of student learning and staff teaching but without jeopardising the relations that constitute a community.

Given these values, a human-centred learning community would apply the following principles to governance:

a   ensuring in the long term that the school's teaching practices are aligned with human-centred values;
b   upholding the school's overall accountability (by holding the Principal or head teacher to account);
c   supporting the ongoing development of a human-centred culture;
d   promoting the participation of parents and other members in the learning community;
e   nurturing democratic and collaborative values;
f   underlining continuity, consistency and constancy in teaching quality and in the experience of students;
g   ensuring long-term alignment to human-centred values.

School governance will be aimed primarily at ensuring that the school's educational vision, practices and strategic direction are aligned with the human-centred values introduced in Chapter 1. In other words, the first principle of governance is to ensure that the educational processes are aimed at the holistic development of the young people.

Upholding the school's overall accountability

The governance of the school will be focused on supporting, overseeing and holding the Principal or head teacher to account for all the processes necessary for the children's holistic learning and well-being. This includes financial sustainability, teaching practices, the school's educational vision, the staff's professional development and well-being and the maintenance of the buildings.

Supporting ongoing development of a human-centred culture and ethos

Good governance lies in the ongoing development of a human-centred culture within the school. This will help ensure coherence among the different stakeholders, including the trustees, governors, the Principal, the teachers, staff and parents.

Promoting the participation of parents and others in the learning community

Good school governance requires the participation of parents in the education of their children. The school regards itself as a learning community and the parents are members of that community.

Nurturing democratic and collaborative values

Human-centred governance aims to nurture democratic and collaborative values. These values include constructive relationships, mutual trust and dialogue. At the same time, as we outline later in this chapter, the various stakeholders will respect each other's different responsibilities.

Underlining continuity, consistency and constancy in the qualities of care, teaching and learning

Good governance will develop policies that stress transparency, continuity, consistency and constancy in accountability. It will also lead to less bureaucracy and increased efficacy. These recommended broad principles would need to be shared by all members of the school community.

Governance processes

So far we have characterised the values and broad principles of human-centred governance. Now we must turn to the governance processes.

Setting the school's strategic direction

The primary task of the governors is to set the school's strategic framework. This includes ensuring the school has a long-term human-centred vision, which underpins the strategic priorities, the aims and objectives of the school and the policies and plans for achieving them.

To ensure the advancement of the school's educational vision, the governors are responsible for launching a development plan and for reviewing and renewing it annually. The strategic goals of the development plan are to be identified by the governors and the school Principal through surveys, dialogues and consultation amongst the stakeholders.

The development plan will spell out the educational standards to which the school should conform, and the responsibilities of the different stakeholders of the school. It will suggest ways to monitor and evaluate ongoing progress in achieving the goals.

Openness, respect and transparency

A human-centred school promotes open and respectful communication as well as clarity and agreement regarding the different stakeholders' responsibilities. This requires transparency in its processes. For instance, all school policies will be the fruit of community-wide consultation. The more open, respectful and transparent the governing processes, the more empowered the members of the community will feel to participate in the school.

The governance of the school occurs at three levels. These levels are not hierarchical; instead, these levels describe different responsibilities within the school community.[2]

First, there is the daily operation of the school. This is the direct responsibility of the Principal. This means that any person who has an executive function in the school shall report to, be accountable to and be appointed by the Principal. The Principal is accountable to the governors.

Second, there is the process of defining school policies and short- and medium-term objectives. This is the responsibility of the Principal and his or her management team, who are directly responsible for achieving the objectives of the school.

Third, there is the responsibility for ensuring that the policies and objectives accord with the intentions or vision that founded the school. This is the responsibility of the governors, who are legally responsible for the school and are held accountable to the educational authorities.[3] The governors set the school's developmental priorities and appoint the Principal. The governors delegate to the Principal the task of monitoring the running of the school and they are not directly involved in day-to-day operational matters, except in exceptional circumstances.

Each of the three groups will respect the remits of others and will follow the processes of reporting and decision-making, which are clearly articulated in a school manual.

Democracy, participation and three-year review

The school is a community of stakeholders who share a common educational vision, but who take different responsibilities in directing the school and in engaging members of the community.

To ensure the participation of all, the governors create institutional spaces for dialogue so that diverse ideas can be integrated into the decision-making and policy-making. The Principal finds ways to collaborate with parents and other community members in the day-to-day running of the school.

The school engages with all members of the community so that they can share the vision, values and ethos of a HCE. As families come and go as their children leave the school, we propose that every three years there should be a whole-school process to revisit and re-engage with the vision through a whole-community dialogue. This three-yearly re-envisioning is not aimed at making changes. Rather, it is intended for community members to understand the human-centred vision.

For similar reasons, the governors will convene open meetings for all parents and other members of the community, including the students, at least once a term so that they can participate in forming the policies and objectives of the school.

Holding the Principal to account

The governors appoint a Principal who is committed to the school's human-centred vision. The heart of good governance in any human-centred school consists in supporting and strengthening the leadership of the Principal and holding him or her to account for the day-to-day running of the school as well as enabling the personal and professional development of teachers.

In a later section ('Qualities of the governors'), we provide a provisional list of the Principal's responsibilities. Holding the Principal to account does not merely mean ticking off the list of tasks and ensuring satisfactory completion of them. Instead, holding the Principal to account means nurturing and supporting the Principal's own personal and professional development and well-being.

Ensuring progress through ongoing evaluation and review

The governors set a framework for checking the overall progress of the school against its objectives and aims, and in light of this, they establish the development plan. Any school needs evidence for assessing the qualities of its educational practices but a human-centred school will rely on alternatives to high-stakes testing. It will review and evaluate itself through very different lenses. One of the tasks of the governors is to develop a framework for bringing these lenses together. There are broadly five such lenses.

The first is the different kinds of learning review, feedback, evaluation and report that we have already discussed in Chapter 5. These are integral to the school's overall teaching and learning practice.

The second is the accountability of the Principal to report to the governing body regularly on how he or she has reviewed and evaluated the school's processes. We will discuss the Principal's own professional development review as a separate topic.

The third is the development plan framework, which spells out key milestones in the school's progress and the practical signs that these have been reached. In most cases, the development plan objectives are tied to the Principal's own professional development focus on ensuring consistent progress of the school.

The fourth consists in surveys, feedback and evaluative conversations with staff, parents, other community members and the students. This requires that the governors develop ways of questioning, facilitating and listening to the relevant conversations. This lens also provides the opportunity to locate the school's aims within the experiences of the larger community it serves.

The last lens is the governors' own self-reflections on the school's progress, both individually and as a group. These reflections include each governor's analysis of his or her experiences of engaging in the governance processes.

When these distinct lenses are woven into a coherent framework, they form a rich tapestry of the community's life and the hub of its governance.

Governors' meetings

In this section, we will provide a standard description of governors' meetings.

At the start of the academic year, the governors spend a day together to plan, discuss and agree on the school's development plan. Once this is done, the governors meet once a term, and these meetings are convened by the Clerk to the governors, who sends written notice of the meeting, a copy of the agenda and meeting materials at least seven working days in advance of the meeting to the following persons: to all governors, the Chair and the Principal. This is standard procedure. Likewise, all meeting decisions are clearly minuted by the Clerk and the minutes are approved by the governors and signed by the Chair at the following meeting. The final minutes are made available to the school community.

The school's annual budget for the next school year is approved during the first half of the summer term, and the school's annual accounts are inspected and reviewed during the governors' meeting in the autumn term before being audited.

For any vote at a meeting, there must be at least fifty per cent of the governors present.

Occasionally, there are emergency decisions to be made in between meetings, in which case:

- all governors are informed of the issue by email;
- all responses are recorded and shared with all governors;

- the Chair of the governors can make emergency decisions if supported by three governors;
- in extreme circumstances, the Chair of the governors can make a decision if supported by the Principal.

In addition to regular full governing body meetings, there are the meetings of individual workgroup meetings to discuss themes and matters within different domains of governance. Workgroups are often formed in the following five domains:

- *Teaching and learning.* Governors in this workgroup will oversee the school's teaching and learning practices, including curriculum, pedagogy, feedback and review, as well as the staff's personal and professional development and well-being. The Principal and/or the Deputy Principal is always part of this workgroup, and it is essential that the workgroup is led by a governor who has a background in education and who has a sound understanding of human-centred approaches.
- *Special education needs (SEN).* Governors in this workgroup must have received, in principle, general training in SEN issues that confront the school. The school's SEN coordinator is part of this workgroup.
- *Safeguarding.* Governors in this workshop will oversee the school's practices in protecting young people from maltreatment, preventing impairment of their health or development, ensuring safe and effective care of all young people and maximising their life opportunities. All governors should receive training in safeguarding young people's interests, and governors in this particular group should be aware of all the vulnerable students in the school, paying special attention to ensure their safety and equal opportunity for access to education.
- *Staff development and relationships.* Governors in this workgroup will oversee the practices that support the development of all staff members in the school and that facilitate the relationships amongst them. The tasks administered by the governors include recruitment and selection of staff, contracts of employment, pay, benefits and conditions of work, staff relations, adjustment to change, and so on. The leading governor of this workgroup should be familiar with employment law, and the workgroup and the Principal should have access to professional advice relating to personnel, staff well-being and relationships.
- *Finance and resources.* Governors and associates in this workgroup will oversee the school's budget, spending and the management of resources. Strategies will be proposed in order to ensure the school's financial stability and sustainability. This workgroup will liaise closely with the Chair of the governors and the Principal. Ideally, both should be members of this workgroup.

Individual governors will be responsible for heading different workgroups with the relevant associates. The workgroup meetings will follow a similar pattern to the governors' meeting in its structure and ways of convening:

- Each workgroup should meet once a term before the full governors' meeting.
- The workgroup meetings are attended by the relevant governors, the Principal and the relevant associates.

- Each workgroup should appoint a chair and a clerk to convene the meeting, take and distribute minutes.
- The chair of each workgroup will report at the governors' meeting on the progress made within a particular aspect of the school's work.

Furthermore, governors convene other forms of meetings which provide opportunities for all members of the community to be part of the governing processes and to participate in decision-making.

Open Forum: An Open Forum is held termly, inviting all members of the community to share experiences, voice concerns, discuss matters of interest and create opportunities for mutual learning. As the name suggests, an open forum provides an open space where there is no predetermined agenda. The space is held safely by a professional facilitator to ensure listening, participation in the conversations and dialogue.

Topic-specific meetings: These meetings are also held termly, inviting all members of the community to discuss a specific topic within the school. This could be a newly introduced pedagogic strategy, a concern about the risk of drug use amongst young people in the school or an opportunity to take the young people to workplaces within the community for exploration. The Chair of the governors or the Principal will prepare the agenda for the meeting, together with a brief description of the topic to be discussed. The objectives of these meetings are to inform and engage the community in matters significant for the school.

Governing bodies

The governors are the leaders of the school community. Sometimes, a school may have a board of trustees who act as the directors of the company, who delegate the responsibilities of running the school to the governors and who act as the management board. In this case, both bodies will work together to ensure that the school achieves its stated mission and objectives, as well as to warrant compliance with the laws of the country. They have a duty of care to make sure that the school is governed with due diligence, and must ensure that the school is solvent and has long-term financial sustainability. The trustees or the governors have limited financial liability for the school in the event of its being wound up and hence, in most countries the trustees or the governors have indemnity insurance.

In this handbook, we will focus our discussion of governing bodies on the governors only.

Composition of the governing body

The governors are recruited from a wide range of school contacts including staff, parents and others from the local community. The school should advertise both locally and nationally. The governors are selected on the basis of their personal background, professional attributes, their knowledge and competences, and above all, their commitment to the school's mission and ethos. They need the ability to facilitate the development of a learning community. Sometimes, governors are chosen for their standing within the local community. Generally, governors have expertise in domains such as education, finance, organisational administration, laws, public relations and marketing.

The Chair of the governors provides new governors with an induction process. Governors are encouraged to attend relevant professional training which takes place outside of the school, such as that organised by the local authority.

The total number of governors should be between seven and nine individuals, including at least:

- the Principal (on an 'ex-officio' basis)
- two parents
- two specialists
- one member of staff
- two or more community members.

A governor's full term is normally three years, which is renewable after completion of the term. It is better that changes to the governing body are staggered; this helps to ensure the continuity of the founding vision and values of the school.

The Chair of the governors should be appointed by agreement amongst the governors and should oversee the recruitment, appointment and induction of new governors

The responsibilities of the governors and the Principal

We are aware that school governance is regulated differently depending on the country and region in which the school is located. The list of responsibilities highlighted here is based on the British government's guidelines for school governors; therefore, they serve merely as a general reference point.

The school governors may be responsible for:

- the recruitment and appointment of the Principal;
- guarding the school's vision and ethos, and overseeing the school's strategic direction (e.g. by overseeing the setting of strategies and priorities in the development plan and monitoring its progress);
- the school's overall accountability to relevant national regulatory bodies;
- ensuring the school's financial viability (e.g. by approving the annual budget and accounts prepared and proposed by the Principal and the school's financial director, arranging for an annual audit and monitoring spending);
- approving and monitoring the school's policies;
- supporting the Principal's professional development;
- monitoring the school's finance in accordance with its annual budget;
- co-opting associates[4] (parents, staff and other members of the community) to serve on one or more committee(s)/workgroup(s).

Concerning a Principal's responsibilities, we want to similarly emphasise that these are differentially specified depending on the country and region in which the school is located. The list of responsibilities highlighted here is based on the British government's guideline for school head teachers and therefore, these can only be regarded as broad guidelines.

The primary responsibility of a Principal is to ensure the overall smooth running of the school, including:

- overseeing the admissions of the students;
- developing teaching and learning practices in accordance with the human-centred vision;
- ensuring the practices of the teachers and other staff members are aligned with the school's mission and aims;
- recruiting and employing all staff members;
- facilitating the work of the teachers through collaboration and co-creation;
- implementing all educational policies and processes;
- overseeing the school's finances and other resources;
- ensuring the school's commitment to equal opportunity, inclusion and participation;
- nurturing the learning community;
- liaising and communicating with parents and the wider community;
- any other aspects of the day-to-day running of the school.

Another major responsibility of the Principal is to ensure students' well-being, the richness and diversity of their educational experiences within the broader aim of their holistic development. Within this category of responsibility, the Principal will be:

- overseeing curriculum development;
- supervising the ongoing development of pedagogy;
- ensuring students' well-being;
- caring for and safeguarding the young people's holistic interests, including meeting students' special educational needs;
- overseeing educational evaluation with regard to (1) the students' ongoing progress, (2) the quality of staff's teaching and learning, and (3) the overall experiences of students and teachers.

Another important responsibility of the Principal is providing for and offering support to the teachers' personal and professional development. Within this key responsibility, there are a number of significant tasks, such as:

- initiating ongoing dialogue and reflection amongst the teaching staff, on teachers' practices (with the view to enabling improvement);
- overseeing teachers' in-service training;
- providing opportunities for teachers' training within and without the school;
- fostering a culture of mutual support and peer learning within the staff team.

In addition to the above key responsibilities, the Principal is also answerable to the governors, and therefore she or he reports regularly to the governors on all aspects of the school's progress, including the advancement made towards the goals and objectives identified in the development plan, by:

- providing a report to each governors' meeting;
- providing a termly update on progress;
- providing an annual full report on the progress of the development plan;
- integrating the goals and objectives of the development plan with the Principal's own professional development plan.

In summary, through this list we wish to stress that a Principal is accountable to the governors for the responsibilities for the school, large and small, and the Principal acts on any (reasonable) directions specified by the governors.

Qualities of the governors

The ideal candidates for governors are those who are best able to understand the human-centred vision and who have the professional capacity to see what this vision means practically for the ethos, policies and practices of the school. Therefore, the following qualities, skills and capabilities are among the most desirable for governors who work in a human-centred school:

a   deep understanding of HCE;
b   professional background and experience to apply this understanding practically and wisely in a diverse learning community within the context of contemporary society;
c   dedication to nurture and support HCE;
d   expertise and experience in general management and governance;
e   capabilities to communicate to the wider society about the human-centred vision.

In other words, the ideal person for the post of governor is someone who:

a   cares about young people and their education;
b   cares about the growth and development of teachers and other staff;
c   has the capacity to listen to the voices of all members of the learning community;
d   has the capacity to oversee the school's finances and long-term development in accordance with its educational vision;
e   has the capacity to make difficult decisions if the school strays from the original vision, and who has the sensitivity and care to explain those decisions in a transparent fashion.

Although we have listed these desirable personal qualities for school governors, we do recommend that when a school community is brought together for the purpose of revisiting the school's educational vision and deciding on the kind of community everyone wishes to develop, the question about the qualities of the governors be raised at the same time. This would enable the community to own the definition of these qualities.

However, as we have shown, there is a bottom line: in a human-centred learning community, the school governors and the Principal work closely together, not in a hierarchical relationship but more in a collaborative and co-creative relationship despite the fact that the latter reports to the former .

Collaboration and co-creation

As a human-centred school is also a learning community, it is essential that the governance processes integrate collaboration and co-creation. We single this out as a separate process because it is seldom included in conventional governance practice.

Insofar as learning occurs as a relational activity in which students and adults collaborate they are not only partaking in and heightening each other's experiences of learning, but they are also co-creating meaning and re-imagining themselves in an ongoing dialogue of being and becoming. However, when applying such relational processes to governance processes, we are likely confronted with manifold complexities and challenges.

Collaboration requires respect for the individual's capacity to care for, engage with, and contribute to the growth and development of the learning community. It also entails the hope that by taking part in a synergetic process one joins with others in becoming an agent of change.

The aim of co-creation is to enrich governance processes by involving all members of the community in identifying values and objectives and aligning them with the school's decision-making. Co-creation transforms each member of the community into an active partner for governing the school, and it shapes the way the school innovates and achieves its vision and educative ends.

In collaboration and co-creation, there are myriad voices, intentions, meanings, responsibilities and identities. The main key to properly attending to and coalescing these diversities is the quality of the relationships within the community. The necessary processes must satisfy at least five criteria:

1   being a collective process towards shared creativity;
2   being inclusive of all stakeholders in the learning community through respect, engagement and listening;
3   being effective, balanced and interesting;
4   being realistic and practical in terms of the community's expectations, that is, the processes ought to nurture enthusiasm and motivation without stimulating false or unrealistic expectations; and
5   being directed at a clear end-point. In other words, these processes need to culminate in a simple and clear document that expresses the community's intention to put into practice the HCE vision as far as circumstances allow.

For instance, the strategic goals of the development plan are identified through listening to and consulting with all the stakeholders of the community, through

•   an end-of-year whole-school survey to identify gaps in the previous year's development plan;
•   a termly Open Forum to consult with stakeholders about emergent goals and needs;
•   teachers' and pupils' in-class discussions about the development plan focus;
•   a community meeting specially dedicated to reviewing the development plan.

Collaboration and co-creation depend on strong relationships, which are further enriched and nurtured through ongoing conversations between the community members/stakeholders. The interests of the community are served not only by the frequency of meetings and interactions but also by the quality of the relationships.

Accountability through supporting professional development

Supporting the Principal's and teachers' professional development is an important aspect of the governors' pursuit of accountability. Traditional 'teachers' performance management' is a conventional phrase that tends to stress hierarchical relationships that regard teaching as performance, thereby separating it from the teacher as a person. In contrast, a human-centred school adopts an appreciative approach to teachers' practices in order to help them review, evaluate and further develop their teaching and learning.

Framing regular review and evaluation from an appreciative perspective can indeed consolidate and reinforce teachers' talents and strengths, and can enable teachers to explore how they can develop further.

Similar points apply to the review of the Principal. Two or three governors will work with the Principal to support his or her professional development. For the teachers, teaching assistants and other support staff, the review team would consist in the Principal, Deputy Principal and senior members of staff.

This review team must communicate clearly to the teachers about the structure of such review. The structure would usually include regular visits to the classroom, dialogic conversations on the teachers' practices, and suggestions as to how to experiment with new ideas and pedagogical approaches. This last aspect is connected to the teachers' own reflections and research.

Appreciative practices require the reviewers to be excellent listeners. When a teacher feels listened to deeply, then he or she will feel trusted and empowered to reflect more deeply about her own practices. Similarly, the review team should be skilled in dialogue because dialogue defines the way the learning community comes together and strengthens relationships. Listening and dialogue can also create a ripple effect, through which teachers adopt the same approach to reviewing the students' work and progress.

As we've noted, when a leadership team lives the human-centred values, the school becomes a nurturing place characterised by love, care, respect, and trust. Correspondingly, in such a culture, teachers can be more open and reflective about their work; they can have courage to be more self-critical and become more daring in taking risks when setting up their own teaching and learning objectives. Teachers who know that the review process is grounded in the appreciation of their work are less afraid of being vulnerable or making mistakes in exploring new things.

This approach to reviewing practices is an expression of care and compassion in which reviewers engage authentically with teachers and with the goodness in their actions.

Conclusion

In the UK, school governors have the same broad responsibilities as company directors and charitable trustees. The Principal's position is akin to that of the Chief Executive Officer.

The primary task of the governors is to set the strategic direction of the school, based on a human-centred vision. They do this by delegating to the Principal and holding the Principal to account for developing educational and other practices and operations of the school.

Good quality governance is the key to the school enjoying an ethos of participation and collaboration, as well as a culture of clear responsibility and accountability. Governance consists fundamentally in values. With good governance, these values are lived in the day-to-day processes of the school.

In this chapter, we have presented a human-centred approach to governance that stresses the values, principles and processes of the governors. By engaging, collaborating and co-creating with the wider community, the governors motivate everyone involved, including the students, to strive for the educational vision of the school.

It is clear that a human-centred approach to governance is not to follow regulations, nor is it to stick rigidly to self-imposed policies. Instead, the governors follow a way of being that empowers others in the school to nurture the learning community.

Notes

1 We thank the staff of Lewes New School in the south of England for sharing their vision of a human-centred approach to governance and governing processes. For more details about how the Lewes New School's governance operates, please see www.lewesnewschool.co.uk.
2 In most schools, these different levels of responsibility are reflected in the levels of remuneration – those who hold more responsibilities are remunerated at a relatively higher rate; but there are schools that actually provide equal pay to all regardless of the levels of responsibility, such as Sands School in England.
3 Some schools have a board of trustees, but most schools simply have governors.
4 Associate members are not governors and they are not recorded in the instrument of government. Associates can attend full governing body meetings but may be excluded from any part of a meeting where the business being considered concerns a member of school staff or an individual student. They are appointed for a period of between one and two years and can be reappointed at the end of their term of office.

Chapter 8

Integrating human-centred education

Overview

In this chapter, we bring together some of the different aspects of human-centred education (HCE) explained in this handbook, and we describe five key steps/processes to guide schools that are interested in embracing a human-centred vision.

The key themes discussed in this chapter include:

- redesigning the school as a community;
- policies, strategies and practice guidelines;
- implementing a human-centred curriculum;
- nurturing a human-centred culture;
- holistic teacher development.

A school does not automatically become a community of humans by merely having an ethos of care. It requires processes whereby leaders, staff members, students, parents and others in the community interrogate the purposes of education and imbibe this culture. The values of the school need to be shared, consolidated and revisited throughout the school's journey. A well-thought-out, whole-school approach is a communal project of constructing a culture.

Once the school decides to adopt a human-centred vision, it will sensitise the staff and provide training to the teachers. The most important training that the teachers need is in shifting the mindset away from the conventional way of teaching which is subject-based and content-oriented, towards a relationship-centred and care-focused pedagogy. The training will help teachers to recognise that a human-centred approach requires a personalised curriculum, formative feedback and appreciative evaluation.

Redesigning the school as a community

As we have shown in this handbook, HCE is a values-based innovative vision. It offers practical possibilities to embed human values in the day-to-day processes of a school.

When redesigning a school, a good starting point is to reflect on what kind of educational vision and ethos the school ought to have. Although all schools will already have articulated an educational vision in broad terms, nevertheless, we propose that a school wanting to adopt HCE would benefit from a reappraisal of its vision. It would need to define collectively in general terms how a human-centred approach might be put into practice.

We suggest starting with a series of dialogues that seeks to bring together school leaders and community members, including parents and students, to understand fully the values, concepts and ideas underlying the HCE vision. The deeper and richer the dialogue, the more likely that the community will embrace a human-centred approach in ways that are appropriate for its specific needs and realities.

Understanding the vision

Before commencing the design process, the school community needs to understand better what HCE is and how it works. Therefore, we would suggest a transition period to help all members of the school community, including parents, to understand the human-centred approach. During this time, students, staff and parents participate in workshops to grasp how the school might change under the new approach. It is essential for a successful implementation that the members of the school community understand well the principles and key features of HCE.

Explanatory workshops can focus on topics such as:

- human-centred values in schools;
- the nature of whole-person learning;
- the human-centred curriculum;
- pedagogy based on care and guidance;
- the nature of a human-centred learning community;
- creating a culture of care in schools.

In the appendices of this handbook, we include some examples of learning communities that have tried to put human-centred ideas into practice.

Planning

In a human-centred learning community, the vision, ethos and overall strategy are developed through dialogue amongst all stakeholders of the school. As we saw in Chapter 7, school governors design the processes for arriving at a statement of vision, ethos and strategy that the community can agree to. These processes are intended to make deep changes to the school's educative practices along the lines discussed in Chapter 1 of this handbook.

To begin, the school team will work together to develop (1) a vision statement, (2) a statement of ethos and (3) a statement of strategy. A vision statement defines the values and direction in which the school intends to develop. A statement of ethos defines the character of the school as a community in its everyday life and, in particular, the nature of the relationships amongst the people involved. A statement of strategy defines how a school is going to change in order to become a human-centred learning community without going into detail.

There are many different routes to these statements. In Chapter 7, we made some proposals for schools already committed to a human-centred project. Here are some suggestions for schools embarking on the journey.

School values assessment

Every school has a unique culture. However, parents, teachers and administrative staff often have different perceptions of the culture. The school values assessment (SVA, see the Barrett Values Centre) helps highlight to what extent the perceptions of these three groups are similar or different. The results can generate deep and meaningful conversations about the purpose and strategy of the school and about the well-being of staff and students. The assessment also provides an overview of what the members of a community see as important in education. It is particularly helpful for the school community to develop a statement of values.[2] It is a first step towards a road map for change aligned to human-centredness.

Whole-school survey

All staff, students and parents will complete a whole-school survey. Such a survey is initiated by the governors. It could be completed anonymously in the form of a questionnaire, online or on paper. In communities where there is no access to online facilities, it may require one-on-one, face-to-face interviews. The result will give an overview of the students', staff and parents' experiences of the school's culture and its educational policies. The insights from the survey will serve to help the school identify gaps in its practices and highlight the needs for change. The survey emphasises what is desirable for the culture of the school.

The community might base its statement of ethos on the emerging ideas from the survey. It enables the school to align its values, principles and ethos with its teaching practices. In Chapter 7, we showed how these would feed into the school's strategies through the goals and objectives of the school's development plan.

Facilitated dialogues

In order for the school to come to agreed statements on vision, ethos and strategy, it is important to schedule facilitated dialogue. In Chapter 7, we offered a discussion of school-wide visioning to show how facilitated dialogues are key to the co-creation of a learning community. Dialogue sessions involve all community members, including governors, staff, students and parents. Since such meetings are likely to be large, they will need some planning to establish a systematic agenda and they will need to be facilitated professionally. They will bear in mind the findings of the SVA and the whole-school survey. Facilitated dialogue can enable the community to frame an initial statement of the school's vision and ethos. They allow members of the community to agree on core values that can be used to guide policy-making and to agree on the broad strategy for bringing the human-centred approach into the school.

Appreciative inquiry sessions

Facilitated dialogues might be supplemented with a community-wide meeting based on the appreciative inquiry method. Appreciative inquiry is a process that focuses on what is already working rather than on what is going wrong. This principle is inherent in all good human relationships. Most of us have experienced an appreciative moment that has changed our lives. Community-wide appreciative inquiry can help identify ways in which the school's practices are already aligned with a human-centred approach, and what else needs to be done.

Table 8.1 (Re)Visioning processes

Processes	Description	Time commitment
School values assessment	This is a direct way of obtaining an overview of what members of the community see as important values. The survey can be completed online.	20–30 minutes for each person to complete the survey. Professional help is needed to analyse the survey data and come to conclusions.
Whole-school survey	To be completed by all staff and students. The survey result will give an overview of these individuals' experiences of the school's culture and educational policies. The survey can help identify gaps in practices and needs for change.	20–30 minutes for each person to complete the survey. Professional help is needed to analyse the survey data and come to conclusions.
Facilitated dialogue	Dialogue helps deepen the community's understanding of the values and agree on common principles that will guide the school's teaching and learning practices.	90 minutes each.
Appreciative inquiry sessions	The school's community comes together to reflect on what is working well in the present system and how to build on these strengths.	Half day, using the appreciative inquiry approach.[1]
Consolidation processes	These are smaller to provide opportunities for parts of the school community to consolidate their understanding of the vision.	60 minutes each.

Consolidation processes

After the above processes, smaller fora are necessary to enable specific groups of stake-holders to consolidate their understanding of particular aspects of the vision. These fora will translate understandings from the different processes into a set of draft policy proposals. These documents will then be subject to the whole-school community consultation and approval.

Table 8.1 summarises these different approaches to the process of (re)visioning.

For most current secondary schools, given the pressures of exams it would seem an impossible luxury to devote time to processes such as those recommended above. That is precisely the reason why it is important to reflect on the needs of the community so that education becomes truly relevant to the students' and community's life and well-being. Seen from Table 8.1, these processes may not seem so impossible in terms of time commitment. The key is for the community to recognise the necessity of change.

Policies, strategies and practice guidelines

Once commitments are received from the staff, parents and students towards an emerging shared vision, the next step would be to establish some 'architecture', which would include the governing principles of the community. For example, the school may need to provide training to teachers to develop their capacity to work closely with young people, or employ those who have already had such training.

When the above step is completed and the school vision, ethos and overall strategy are clarified, a school can begin to specify in more detail the practical implications for day-to-day activities and relationships. These are often in the form of policies and practice guidelines.

Most schools have policies regarding teaching and community life. Developing such policies can be a slow process, and the school governors or leadership team tend to liberate the staff from the burden of this time-consuming exercise. However, from a human-centred perspective, it is necessary that such processes involve the teaching staff and other stakeholders depending on the issue at hand. This is an important part of building a learning community. Take the curriculum as an example. A human-centred curriculum is radically different from the traditional conception of a school curriculum. There needs to be school-wide conversations about the new curriculum. Without them, the school would not be a community. There are many other conversations crucial for developing the school as a community: How do the staff work together to employ existing talents and specialist expertise within the team? What additional training is necessary? How to arrange the teaching and learning spaces in view of the current resources?

The development of school policies needs to be grounded in a good understanding of the human-centred approach and, in particular, an appreciation of what constitutes holistic development for young people. For instance, what students need for their self-development is an issue that has to be addressed on an individual basis. This understanding will be reflected in the teaching policies, curriculum and pedagogy guidelines, as well as in ongoing teacher training and professional development.

Policy discussions might be based on improving, transforming and adding to existing school practices. New policy tends to be abstract and less applicable to the daily life of the teachers, students and the community as a whole. Policies are guidelines for practice.

The school will ensure that policies are regularly updated. This requires planning for ongoing dialogue about human-centred policies within the school community. We discussed how to develop school policies so that they are a reflection of human-centred values in Chapter 7.

Implementing a human-centred curriculum

Once a school has committed to becoming more human-centred and has taken its first steps towards becoming a learning community, it will go through the policy changes described in the previous section.

Whilst it is doing that, a team in the school needs to plan the implementation of the human-centred curriculum. Someone needs to work on a complete proposal to put to the school governors. In Chapter 3, we described a fully human-centred curriculum. Few schools, if any, would be able to put this curriculum into effect all in one go. There needs to be a process of transitioning to the new curriculum. In this process, there are some essential and difficult points to bear in mind.

First, what we described in Chapter 3 is only an outline or framework for a curriculum. For example, we characterised some of the key elements of Cognitive Time and of Group Time, but we didn't provide a definite schedule. Similarly, we didn't specify the content of General Knowledge Time and of Exploration Time. Each school would need to do this for itself. We cannot offer specific recommendations in this handbook independent of context. Each school will be different.

Second, the school will face a conflicting set of demands with respect to how much to change. On the one hand, in most countries, there is enormous pressure from the demands of a national curriculum and of public exams. On the other hand, the school wants to become a human-centred community. One of the main pressure points in the new curriculum will be Specialist Subject Time because this is where the young people study traditional subject areas. How much time does the school need to dedicate each week to these traditional subject areas? How many subject areas should the students typically be taking? What are the in-house requirements for a student to sit a public exam?

Third, the school can approach the same issue from the other side: How much time can the school dedicate to the new human-centred curriculum elements? In this regard, we have stressed the primary importance of the three pillars: Direction Time, Cognitive Development Time and Group Time. We regard these as the minimal essentials for a human-centred curriculum. Towards the end of Chapter 3, we provided a sample weekly timetable to show that it is feasible to introduce these and other human-centred elements into the curriculum. However, this was only a sample. The school will need to think through the relevant issues for its own particular context. For instance, it will need to ask, can we provide mentoring sessions for individual students on a weekly basis? Can we afford the additional staff? If not, what can we do and is it still meaningful? Similar questions will arise for the other curricular elements, such as Group Time.

Fourth, the school will probably want to phase in the new curriculum elements bit by bit. It is wise to see what works and, if it doesn't, to consider why. Once the school has decided how much of the curriculum elements it might introduce then it can plan how to transition to that new curriculum over, for instance, a three-year period.

Fifth, there is another important planning element. The school will need to consider the time demands on teachers and other staff members. We hope that the process of phasing in a human-centred curriculum will be an exciting one, and that the school will not make it too stressful in its wish to be ambitious. Nevertheless, during the transition period, there will be extra demands on teachers and other staff. Furthermore, what will the working week typically look like for the teachers after the changes have been put into place? Are there too many demands on teachers' time? How can we simplify?

Nurturing a human-centred culture

A human-centred learning community is characterised by its relationships. It is vitally important that all members of the school community treat one another with care. Caring, respectful, authentic relationships characterise the culture of the school. In such conditions, young people are more likely to develop holistically and teachers are more likely to feel that their work is meaningful.

We have several suggestions concerning how to nurture a caring culture.

First, we suggest that students and staff are allocated time to reflect on key questions regarding how they themselves, and the school as a whole, might improve and become more human-centred. This time is both reflective and creative. It is reflective because it is a review critical of the relationships amongst members of the community and of the culture of the school. It is also creative because it is an opportunity to imagine new ways of fulfilling human-centred aims.

The leadership team might want to propose questions like these at a school meeting for discussion:

- How do I treat other members of the school community as people?
- Who do I need to be kinder and more considerate towards?
- In what ways are we a real community of people who care for each other?
- How can I help our community to become more caring?
- How can I support and help others better?
- What support and help do I need?
- How can the adults in the school help me and others develop as whole persons?
- What are the specific ways that we as a school can embody human-centred values?
- In what way can the school connect better with the wider community?

Such a process of reflection can provide momentum to the formation of a learning community.

Second, when adults and young people meet in an environment in which they feel equal and free of their roles, this can promote mutual understanding, trust and belonging. Most interactions in schools are driven by an agenda which makes it difficult for students and staff to meet as persons and as equals. Agenda-driven meetings tend to incorporate the power imbalances inherent in the traditional student–teacher dynamic. Opportunities for non-agenda-driven interactions could be incorporated into the timetable to enable relationships to become more friendly and humane.

Third, a weekly democratic school meeting might be built into the schedule. Such a meeting could focus on significant decision-making within the school, such as the use of school buildings, disciplinary processes, the structure of the timetable and the election of a head boy or girl. Members of the school community (adult or young person) might chair these meetings on a rotating basis. They could operate on a one-person, one-vote footing. The meetings would be run so that everyone feels comfortable to speak and that their voices are being heard.

Other ideas include employing new staff through a more democratic selection process, including collaboratively writing job descriptions, forming interview panels made up of staff, students, governors and parents, and making the final selection decision inclusive.

These kinds of democratic processes enable all members of the school community to feel empowered and committed to a common cause. It is in this kind of environment that adults and young people can come to understand each other as people, rather than merely as role occupants. The trust and understanding that is built in this environment will not remain solely in these interactions; it will transform the relationships throughout the school and change people's lives.

Fourth, there might be a regular contemplative session appropriate to the cultural traditions of the community. In many parts of the world, religious rituals and spiritual practices, such as silence, prayers, mediation and mindfulness, are integral to the day-to-day rhythm of the school. These contemplative sessions provide teachers and students with the opportunity to listen to their innermost selves or to dialogue with a divine other. Such sessions may enable individuals to become more mindful and more compassionate.

In a human-centred learning community, relationships are in important regards non-hierarchical. Adults and students treat one another as equally worthy of respect and care. In this manner, everyone is treated as an equal, despite differences in roles. As we have illustrated, such respect is achieved through the structures and processes of the school. The governors and leadership team can foster a culture of equality through these same processes.

For this to work, adults and young people will value one another's whole-person development. For instance, they will care whether others feel fulfilled in their learning and work. For this reason, teachers should be able to be more themselves in the classroom, without the professional reserve that is often expected from teachers. There would be more freedom and opportunities for both staff and students to express their anxieties and hopes, as well as their interests and disinclinations. These would not become the focus of the class, but equally they should not be hidden away. Understanding the perspectives and feelings of one another will help the learning community to become more unified around an ethos of respect and care.

Holistic teacher development

Key to a school's transformation towards being human-centred is that the teaching team embraces the process of transition. This may involve a substantial time commitment. The transition period is a time of experimentation, dialogue and reflection, and only from this can it emerge how the team might best work together. In a human-centred school, the teachers will work in interdependent and mutually supportive ways. Each individual teacher will understand the value and importance of his or her own work and role and how this relates to that of the other teachers. In Chapter 4, we mapped out the different teaching positions and showed how teachers collaborate in a human-centred curriculum.

During this transition period, the leadership will take care to ensure that the process is smooth as well as exciting. In particular, the leadership needs to consider the demands on the teachers throughout this process. The main idea of HCE is that we concentrate our energy on what it is important and valuable. We try to create institutional processes that make this possible on a regular basis. If those same processes become too demanding, then we have defeated the very purpose of the proposed changes. The same point applies to the ideas that we described in Chapter 6 concerning teacher support and training.

Response to concerns

In this chapter, we have drawn together the different threads of a human-centred approach to education and schooling and made suggestions in terms of how schools might begin to implement HCE in their processes. By now, readers are bound to have concerns about such implementation. In this section, we would like to try to allay and answer some of these concerns. In so doing, we will repeat some points made earlier in this handbook and this chapter.

'A human-centred vision is idealistic'

The concern is that the vision outlined in this handbook is idealistic. In reply to this problem, the idea that idealism should be contrasted with and tempered by practical realism is a false one. The two ideas are about two different things and need to exist side by side. They are easy bedfellows. Idealism is about articulating the ideals that should define our direction; that is, where we ought to be heading. Practical realism is about recognising the many difficulties about moving in that direction. One is about ends and the other is about means. We need both, as distinct energies. Increasingly, they tend to be muddled up; education is being hijacked by instrumental rationality and cost-effective analysis. It is time to restore a deeper vision of the aims of education based on human development and well-being. However, this does not mean that a human-centred educational vision is not also a practical philosophy. Its implementation must be rooted in the hard realities of teaching and learning in schools.

'Human-centred education is expensive'

It may be beyond the budget of most schools to apply the HCE curriculum in full, especially because of the regular individual mentoring sessions. However, the HCE curriculum doesn't need to be implemented all at once. The school can introduce the curriculum bit by bit and in accordance with its own resources. HCE is first and foremost an analysis of what education is and from this, a set of suggestions about how it should be carried out. If the community members of a school agree with the HCE vision, then they will find ways to put into practice what is possible within their school. It doesn't need to be all or nothing. It can be introduced progressively and step by step.

'We can't implement human-centred education because we are already overstretched'

Many schools feel overburdened with too much to do. Taking on another huge project would seem like too much. We don't want to advocate HCE for schools that find it difficult to take it on. However, if a school community feels overburdened then they may want to address *this* situation directly. 'Why are we overstretched?', 'Are we able to concentrate on what is most important for the students?', 'How can we feel less overstretched and become less busy?', 'How can we find time for group reflection?', 'How can we find time to get to know each other better?', 'What can we do to make more time for ourselves and for our students?' and 'What are our priorities as an educational institution?'

'The implementation of human-centred education takes too much time'

In this handbook, we have described lots of meetings and workshops. Some are for building the school as a community. Some are to strengthen the support for teachers. Some are to plan collectively the implementation of HCE in the school. A well-planned process of implementing HCE will assign tasks to different groups and it will decide a whole-school process that involves some division of labour. If the process is well-planned, it will not be laborious and chaotic. There are certain decisions that need to be taken in big meetings to ensure that everyone is on board and engaged. There are other decisions that are better taken in smaller meetings. Democracy doesn't mean that everyone decides everything.

'Human-centred education is not for our students'

The concern is that HCE provides a vision that is best suited to students who come from backgrounds that are more privileged, or is less suited for young people who struggle academically. In reply, HCE principles are applicable to young people of all abilities and backgrounds. The central core is to give students attention and care directed at their most important needs. For example, if a student has needs in developing his or her motivation, the Mentor is there to work with him or her and to address this; if the student needs support in paying attention, then the Mentor and Tutor will help the student with this. Students who have emotional needs will have the opportunity to work on these in a safe and professionally facilitated environment with the support of their peers. In addition, all students need the opportunity to grow intellectually, to develop their thinking or cognitive skills. In this way, HCE aims to introduce into the mainstream system alternative educational practices so that the majority of young people benefit from an education that really cares about them.

'Human-centred education takes too much time away from preparation for exams'

We don't belittle the instrumental value of good exam results: as qualifications, they are hugely important for students' future lives. Therefore, it is necessary that students have the opportunity to do as well as they can in these exams. Nevertheless, we have three points to make in reply to this concern for lack of time to prepare for exams. The first is that focusing much attention on the exams and their content doesn't help the student to grow, to become the kind of person who has the self-confidence, the motivation and the intellectual abilities to do well in the exams. Concentrating on the exams is a bit like planning to play a football match without doing any fitness training and team building. The activities needed to grow in physical strength and fitness are quite different activities from those involved in playing a match. Likewise, helping our students to become mentally and emotionally stronger and fitter is a quite different set of activities from preparing for exams. Second, the main aim of educating students is to make them more fully developed and more mature, not simply to provide them with qualification currency or tokens, despite the instrumental value of these. Third, if exam certificates are instrumentally important because they are currency or tokens, remember that this means that they are only *representations* of the good qualities that education aims at. They are like pictures of the goods only. They aren't the real thing.

'Human-centred education will lower our academic standards'

First, please don't identify academic standards with exam results. Exams are one way to measure the standards. A school that has strong academic standards is one in which the students and teachers respect the usually implicit norms that are inherent in the activities of their disciplines. As we saw earlier, there are implicit values in text analysis, art appreciation, mathematical problem-solving and scientific experimentation. Equally, there are implicit values in reading, writing, thinking and creating, which vary according to the context. This is what 'academic standards' means. The essence of academic performance consists in the strengthening of the qualities or virtues that enable our young people to care about and respond to these values. This is why academic standards are integral to HCE. HCE is about the development of the student that requires the development of qualities or virtues. These virtues include those that involve caring more about the values implicit in academic standards. In this sense, HCE should be associated with higher academic standards and not with their lowering. A second point, in fact, is that the apprehension may lie not so much with HCE itself but rather with the way in which it might be implemented. The concern might be that, with less time devoted to the traditional subjects, students will become less academic. This is why we have stressed the importance of teachers challenging the students. Students who are less academically motivated need to be challenged to enable their intelligence to grow, and to nurture their care for this aspect of themselves.

Conclusion

Redesigning the school requires a systemic approach. In this chapter, we have described this process in terms of five steps.

The first is that the school becomes a learning community. A learning community is unified around a common vision and embodies a shared set of values. The more a school community and its members live and embody the values of care and respect, the more such values become the very fabric of the community.

The second is that the school adopts a set of human-centred policies which will guide practice in the school. These policies will need to be agreed on by the community as a whole. To ensure that these policies have a human-centred focus is to align the main aim with the holistic development of the students.

The third step is that the school introduces elements from the human-centred curriculum outlined in Chapter 3, but in accordance with its own conditions and situation. Together with associated relationally enriching pedagogical and evaluative practices, these curriculum elements are there to achieve the main aim of enabling the students to grow more fully as human beings.

The fourth is that the school nurtures a human-centred culture, a culture in which there is no fear: no fear of failure, of authority, of teachers, of punishment and of speaking one's mind. In short, as a human-centred community the school makes a deliberate collective effort to create a culture of caring, respect and mutuality.

The fifth step is that the school introduces institutional processes to train and support its teachers. The objective is that the teachers will relish their newly defined roles within the new curriculum and will welcome the new opportunities for personal and professional development and mutual support.

These steps can take place simultaneously, although we have suggested that the first be regarded as a precondition for the other four.

This handbook constitutes only a starting point for the humanising of the educational system. It describes the changes that a school as an institution would need to undergo to become human-centred. In themselves, such institutional changes do not constitute a transformation of the educational system itself. Even the most HCE-oriented school would still need to comply with the requirements of the national education system, such as the public exams and national curriculum.

This by no means suggests that the HCE philosophy doesn't advocate a transformation of the whole system at its core. However, it also provides practical suggestions for schools who want change, even though they operate within the existing system which they cannot endeavour to change.

Nevertheless, hope does remain. At the micro level, we can change our interactions. At the personal level, we can transform our teaching practices and our relational ways of being. At the institutional level, we can change our teaching roles and we can alter the mission, vision and objectives of a school. Furthermore, as more and more schools embrace a human-centred vision and as more and more communities recount transformative narratives about their young people, then we will come closer to transforming education at the systemic level.

Notes

1 A good example of the appreciative inquiry process can be found at: www.taosinstitute.net/co-creating-schools-of-the-future-through-appreciative-inquiry, or see the book *Appreciative inquiry* by Cooperrider and Whitney (2005).
2 See Appendix 9.4 *School Values Assessment*, developed by Barrett Values Centre, for more details.

Appendices

Overview

In this part of the book, we provide a collection of resources in the form of appendices aimed at offering additional support to schools intending to embrace human-centred education (HCE). It is worth mentioning that despite our best efforts to seek case studies or illustrative examples there are few schools worldwide that truly practise human-centred education (HCE). In fact, if there were many good exemplars of human-centred schools, especially mainstream schools, there wouldn't be such need for us to write this handbook.

However, there are some projects, articles, books, websites and stories that may serve as both stimuli and provide inspirational ideas for schools and teachers. We have grouped these appendices in the following categories:

- case studies illustrating aspects of human-centred education (Appendix 1);
- web-based resources (Appendix 2);
- books and articles (Appendix 3).

The appendices are not exhaustive. Instead, they start a process of building resources that can help illustrate the possibilities of HCE in different parts of the world. The reason why it is difficult to find authentic exemplars that help showcase holistic human-centred approaches to education is because very few secondary schools in the world are able to establish themselves as human-centred learning communities, not due to lack of motivation or interest but as the result of the constraints of high-stakes testing at the end of secondary education and the obligation to teach a prescribed national curriculum.

So it is not surprising that the case studies in Appendix 1 are either small alternative schools, or private or independent schools. Equally, the web-based resources may seem fragmented as some are TED Talks, some are videos of schools, others are educational movements and others still are pedagogical approaches, such as alternative approaches to test-based assessment.

The inclusion of books is also highly selective and we are sure that there are many more similar materials that could be added to our list.

As we have said, these appendices merely serve as a conversation starter, aimed at inspiring more attention to be paid to human-centred approaches to education by educational thinkers, practitioners, researchers, parents and students worldwide. If you are interested in participating in online conversations about HCE, please consult our website, http://humancentrededucation.org.

Appendix 1: case studies of human-centred education

The case studies collected here exemplify some of the qualities that we promote in this handbook. They also illustrate how HCE can be differentially practised depending on the social, cultural and political contexts within which it is conceived and carried out. Few of these schools will actually call themselves 'human-centred schools', apart from Korowal School and Cita Bina Utama School; nevertheless, there are some aspects in their practices that seem to be aligned with a human-centred concern. Therefore, we have chosen carefully which features of each school to include here to showcase HCE.

The way we structure each case study is as follows:

a   the overall values and principles underpinning the school's practice;
b   pedagogical approaches;
c   specific features or programmes;
d   a brief discussion on why the selected features or programmes exemplify human-centredness.

In doing so, we hope that these case studies will help to build a more grounded understanding of how a school might begin to consider teaching and learning in a more human-centred way.

Korowal School in Australia

(http://www.korowal.nsw.edu.au/)

> At Korowal I feel respected, and because of this I want to learn and I have fun when I learn. That is what I think a school should be.
>
> (16-year-old student)

Korowal School (Korowal) is a small private school located in the Blue Mountains just outside of Sydney, Australia. It was founded in 1978 with the aim of providing a human-centred learning environment.

The school explicitly practises human-centred values and principles such as compassion, tolerance, equity, respect, empathy, commitment, resilience and critical thinking. It places a strong emphasis on the quality of human relationships including committed, mutually respectful relationships amongst students, teachers and parents/guardians. This is at the foundation of what Korowal sees as a HCE. Equally, the school regards cultivating the full potential of the whole human being as a central aim of education and that this can only be achieved by educating in a balanced and integrated way: intellectually, creatively, socially, physically, emotionally, ethically and spiritually.

Korowal features a human-scale environment where students, teachers and parents or guardians can be known, understood and valued as individuals. Smaller classes and integrated structure means that teachers, parents and students of all ages can care for each other, balancing the individual and the community. The school considers this way of learning together as socially sustainable.

What make Korowal's practices most akin to a human-centred approach are the two interconnected aspects: one being the respect for each individual students' needs, which enables the school to provide tailored support to each student, and the other being the relationships between the students and the teachers. The school invests time and effort towards developing clear, consistent and committed relationships within which mutual trust and respect can develop. Through this, the students develop self-respect as well as responsibility for oneself and for others and the community.

Each day begins with a morning meeting where the teachers and students converse and discuss things that matter to them. This space sits in between Direction Time and Group Time in the human-centred curriculum. For the adolescents, each class has two teachers who are like Mentors and who stay with the same group of students for four years. This arrangement makes it possible for the teachers to develop a good knowledge about each student and foster a strong relationship with the student. The school also allocates time for teachers to pay attention to and care for each student, providing an optimal opportunity for the young person to develop his or her interests and pathways in learning and growth.

Korowal's approach shows that pedagogy tuned in to the individual student's developmental needs must be located within a school structure that enables the teacher to maintain a continued presence in the student's life, to give time to develop a respectful, caring and humane relationship with the student, and to create space to ensure the possibility for both the adult and the young person to avail oneself to the other in the mutuality of learning. Without a supportive structure, it is impossible to fully integrate human-centred pedagogy.

Colegio Amor in Colombia

(http://www.fundacionamor.org/)

> For me the most important sign is the face of the child. They have the face of happiness, not fear. They are confident and secure.
>
> (A visitor to Colegio Amor)

Colegio Amor is located in the town of Soacha, south-west of Bogotá, Colombia. It was founded in 1988 with the aim of supporting children from refugee parents, displaced and migrant families who suffered during the violence of the civil wars and armed conflicts. The social problems facing the community include unemployment, drug and alcohol abuse, AIDS, gang/street violence and domestic violence.

In this context, Colegio Amor's vision is that education must be aimed at whole-person flourishing, and to enable the flourishing of children and young people an education must begin with affectionate and loving relationships amongst the teachers, students and families; in other words, it is love in action. The school sees that love is the force or energy that activates our livelihood and sustains profound human relationships.

As most of the families have been traumatised in some way during violent conflict, the school believes that the most conducive environment for children's development is one that provides security, protection, love and respect. When these conditions are well met, children can begin to be supported in overcoming the traumas and pressures of their lives and develop into human beings with a firm set of internal and external values and an awareness of their own self-worth, talents and potential.

What brings Colegio Amor's educational efforts close to a human-centred approach is that it sees the aims of education as deeply rooted in the needs of the children as well as in the needs of the community. This concern for each individual student's holistic well-being and the well-being of the community, and the underlying conviction of the interconnectedness and interdependence between the well-being of the individual and that of the community, mark the school's work truly human-centred.

One way of showing care for students' needs is that the school provides them with nutritious snacks because many children are malnourished or are hungry when they arrive at the school in the morning. Similarly, all students are given a school uniform to wear. This is not out of discipline or uniformity, but intends to make sure that all students are clothed properly, with dignity.

Another way of understanding the student's needs are through home visits. As the school supports the students, it simultaneously enhances the community's capacity to improve and strengthen itself. Hence, there is a partnership between the school and the community through the education of the children and young people and the education of adults within the community.

Furthermore, Colegio Amor introduces co-curricular activities to meet the specific needs of the students, which are to do with developing the knowledge, skills and capabilities to overcome the myriad social problems listed earlier. These co-curricular programmes include psycho-therapeutic activities for traumatised students, a micro-enterprise programme for older students, arts and culture experiences to enrich students' emotional well-being, and an 'integral prevention programme' aimed at helping those at risk become aware of the underlying causes of their existing problems (e.g. drug and alcohol abuse, gang culture, sexually transmitted diseases and so on) and their social consequences.

The school's human-centredness lies in its focus on cultivating the individual student's awareness of their own self-respect and self-worth, which further enables them to take responsibility for themselves and later become agents of change and support the growth of the community. This could potentially lead to a virtuous cycle of personal and social transformation.

Bina Cita Utama School in Indonesia

(http://www.bcuschool.com/)

> I have learned that the greatest resource for teaching is found in our heart.
>
> (A participant at the Bina Cita Utama School's teacher training programme)

Opened in 2005, Bina Cita Utama is the first bilingual multicultural school in the province of Central Kalimantan, Indonesia, serving students aged 6 to 17. The name Bina Cita Utama means 'nurturing noble ideals' and the school is dedicated to nurturing the whole person through developing a high-quality, human-centred learning environment, rich and caring relationships and challenging and stimulating educational programmes.

Being a bilingual school with volunteers coming from around the world, the school encourages students to become active citizens who face up to their social and civic responsibilities and to be caring and community-minded, have cultural understanding and demonstrate respect and tolerance for the cultures and habits of others.

One of the important features of the school is what is called 'child-centred pedagogy' where the student is the active participant in the learning process, rather than the passive recipient of a predetermined set of knowledge and information. This child-centred approach recognises that each student has his or her unique pace for learning and growth, and each student has his or her particular character, dispositions and strengths, and by focusing on cultivating each individual's distinct qualities that are suited to their own nature, Bina Cita Utama's pedagogy becomes tailored and personalised rather than one-size-fits-all.

Self-Managed Learning College (SMLC) in Brighton, England

(http://college.selfmanagedlearning.org/)

> A [name of a student] has attended SMLC from age 11 to 16 and has been very happy. She has been allowed to and shown how to manage herself and her learning. She can pursue subjects that interest her and to the level that she wants with the support of the College and its tutors.
>
> (A parent, Self-Managed Learning College)

Founded in 2000, the Self-Managed Learning College in Brighton, south-east of England, is a vibrant learning community that offers a real alternative to schooling. The College provides a small, stimulating and nurturing environment where students can develop their qualities such as confidence, independent learning, inquiry, collaboration and other skills for pursuing lifelong learning and ongoing personal development.

The self-managed learning approach was developed in the late 1970s and has been perfected by the College's founder, Professor Ian Cunningham, and is a structured approach to learning consisting of three core elements: (1) learning agreement, (2) the learning group and (3) the learning community. In exploring the mutuality of learning, self-managed learning promotes both independence and interdependence in developing capacity for learning, responsibility, thought and action. The safety of the learning group and the caring support of the facilitator enable the student to embrace challenges in pursuing their own learning and developmental goals.

The aspect in the College's pedagogy that is closest to a human-centred approach is the way the teachers work with the students through individual mentoring and peer mentoring (for lack of better words).

As illustrated in Box 3.2 of Chapter 3, each learning group dedicates time to the individual who, by considering his or her personal experiences, past, present and future, arrives at learning goals and pathways that are unique to his or her dispositions, interests and life plans. These are captured in a Learning Agreement which the group agrees with the individual student and is referred to when his or her progress is discussed. With the support from the mentor/facilitator and the group, the students can plan, organise and carry out their learning activities and take responsibility for pursuing their personal goals and objectives.

Also included in the Learning Agreement, as we elaborated in Chapter 3, is a set of criteria that characterises the fulfilment of the agreement, for example, what qualities mark the accomplishment of one's learning goals, flavours of the learning experience and evaluative accounts of how these have been achieved. This reflective and evaluative dimension, together with the learning group's and mentor/facilitator's ongoing feedback on the student's progress, ensures that personal developmental goals, curriculum activities, mentoring and pedagogical support, learning feedback and review are integral to the student's overall educational experience.

Thus, learning is highly personalised and each student has his or her own timetable within the overall timetable of the College. Hence, the curriculum also resembles a human-centred idea, in particular, in the Direction Time, Subject Time, Exploration Time and, most importantly, Project Time.

The College's self-managed learning process has been proven to show genuine care for the students' individual needs and respect for their unique learning preferences and paces. The strengths of the group support and the sense of mutuality engendered through this way of working and collaborating, has made the Self-Managed Learning College a true learning community.

Brockwood Park School, England

(http://brockwood.org.uk/)

I feel at Brockwood, it is like a home to me.

(A student)

Brockwood Park School (Brockwood) is an international, co-educational boarding school in the southern English countryside. Inspired by Jiddu Krishnamurti's educational ideas that encouraged the flourishing of the whole person including self-understanding, open-mindedness, intellectual growth, sensitivity, creativity and integrity, the school exhibits human-centredness in its ethos, curriculum design and pedagogy.

The school centres its ethos on a safe, non-competitive setting where the outer environment of natural beauty, the inner environment of tranquillity and peace, and the relational environment of care, respect and love intertwine in making a truly rich and integrated human and humane learning environment.

Seventy students learn the art of living, studying and growing together through relationship, responsibility, care, mutual inspiration, open-ended exploration and an insistence on excellence in all aspects of their learning and development.

The school summarises its five core values as (1) freedom and responsibility, (2) individuality and community, (3) independence and collaboration, (4) expression and rigour and (5) reflection and action. They provide a firm foundation for the students and the teachers to embrace education as a pathway to the flourishing of oneself and the community.

We appreciate most about Brockwood's education from a human-centred perspective its non-instrumental approach to learning and education in general. Learning is an intrinsic end in itself and education is the flowering of the whole, integrated human being. Similar to Direction Time, teachers have conversations with each student throughout the year to explore particular needs, interests and talents, and to identify a balanced programme of study for each individual.

Teaching focuses on creating the spaces within the curriculum to enable the students to pursue, nurture and develop their own interests, paying attention to both depth and breadth in the students' learning experiences and hence, promoting 'excellence' in every way. Whether a student is working on an extended project, writing an essay, composing a piece of music or practising yoga, the students are encouraged to engage with learning through sustained attention, inquiry and diligence.

The school starts each day with a meeting which consists of stillness and inward reflection. This invites each person to be fully present in his or her educative experience throughout the day.

The curriculum features discovery or 'uncovering' rather than the traditional sense of 'coverage', and the school's environments – the physical one with the natural beauty of the gardens and grounds, the inner one of quietude and peacefulness, and the relational one of caring for one another, the community and the world – encourage the students' engagement, participation and collaboration. Instead of being perceived as an authority, teachers work together to foster students' disposition for deep learning, including those of their own.

Brockwood recognises the students' need to leave education with qualifications in order to continue to higher education or workplaces. However, acquiring these qualifications through exams is never considered an objective of education. Instead, for any student who wishes to acquire such qualifications, support is provided but the school does not let passing exams interrupt its main educative activities.

Appendix 2: web-based resources

Below are a few online resources that explore educational ideas, approaches and practices which may have some common features with the kinds of ideas presented in this handbook. These are simply to provide the reader with a glimpse of the kinds of resource available on the Internet that could in some ways support more human-centred approaches. They do not necessarily fully illustrate HCE as such, and we do not want the reader to have that impression that these are so.

www.hsc.org.uk

Like HCE, the Human Scale Education movement emphasises the primacy of caring relationships to meaningful learning, promoting learning environments where young people are known and valued for who they are. It promotes practices which embed processes of appreciative feedback, active inquiry, collegiate sharing of talent and expertise amongst staff and connecting with parents and the wider community. It emphasises the importance of schools having a sense of belonging and community and the importance of an ethos of respect, responsibility and equal value. Human-scale education may include integrated curricula, opportunities to learn in real-world settings, co-construction of learning plans and flexible use of time. This website provides a wealth of resources on relevant literature and schools and other educational endeavours which embody these values.

https://www.youtube.com/watch?v=76WqxjhCrFQ&index=6&list=PLsRNoUx8w3rM478DeXL2PWbV4YnqSSNJJ

(Accessed June 2016)

In this video Matthew Malone, the Secretary of Education in Massachusetts tells the tale of his relationship with one student to emphasise his message about the importance of relationships and love within education.

http://www.holistic-education.net/visitors.htm

According to this introduction from Holistic Education Inc., the purpose of holistic education is to prepare students to meet the challenges of living as well as academic challenges. Holistic education asks what we need to know in order to live good and meaningful lives, believing in the importance of young people learning about themselves and healthy relationships and to develop both socially and emotionally. Like HCE, the holistic education movement emphasises the importance of a young person feeling that their life and learning are meaningful. This website provides links to several articles exploring these ideas further.

http://www.holisticeducationuk.org/

The Holistic Education Organisation (HEO) UK believes that the well-being and development of the child should be at the heart of every educational provision, and that this should be prioritised over national attainment goals and economic ambitions. The organisation promotes educational endeavours which aim to support the development of the whole child, and its website gives details of the main types of educational provision currently available in the UK that promote these holistic values.

http://citl.indiana.edu/resources_files/teaching-resources1/alternatives-to-exams.php

This website draws on the work of Walvood and Anderson (2004) to present some ideas for the types of assignments one might set instead of traditional exams. The University of Indiana encourages its tutors to interrogate the aims of their assessment design and create assignments that are appropriate and creative.

https://www.youtube.com/watch?v=Z5KaKnli6oc

(Accessed June 2016)

This video presentation gives an overview of the nature, design and evaluation process of alternative assessment methods, similar to those described by Walvood and Anderson (2004).

http://bie.org/about/what_pbl

Project-based learning is a teaching method by which students gain knowledge and skills by working for an extended period of time to investigate and respond to an engaging and complex question, problem or challenge. This website gives some details of the kinds of broadly human-centred aspects that project-based learning might include, such as sustained inquiry, student voice and choice, reflection, critique, key knowledge, understanding and skills.

https://www.youtube.com/watch?v=08D0dBGIzYQ

This video gives a short introduction to project-based learning, elucidating the core processes involved in teaching in a project-based way, including how to generate interest in students and choose an appropriate driving question, how to build appropriate knowledge and understanding, how to develop a product/end outcome and the motivational potential of presenting that outcome to an external audience such as parents.

https://www.ted.com/talks/ken_robinson_says_schools_kill_creativity?language=en

In this now well-known and popular TED talk video, Sir Ken Robinson challenges the way young people are educated in the UK and calls for a shift towards creative approaches that equip students for adult life.

https://www.youtube.com/watch?v=gPnuJv3FI3A

(Accessed June 2016)

In this video, Guy Claxton explores the role of creativity in educating young people to be able to flourish in the modern world. He touches on the importance of developing not only knowledge and skills, but also attitudes, values or 'habits of mind' (Dewey) for being able to flourish, such as self-discipline, being a good friend or citizen, moral courage, kindness and creativity. These attitudes or values are reminiscent of the human-centred conception of qualities or virtues.

There are few providers of alternative teacher training along the lines proposed in this handbook. However, the following may be of interest in understanding the kinds of course design or approach that might be appropriate for HCE teacher training.

www.brockwood.org.uk/pdf/teaching_academy2010.pdf

Here are details of a teacher training course run by Brockwood Park School, which encourages participants to revisit the aims of education, the nature of learning, the challenges young people face, the role of the teacher, the importance of relationships and communication and the culture of the learning environment. The training is based on the idea that 'The problem is not what kind of education the child should have, but rather, that the educator needs education' (Krishnamurti).

https://www.mariamontessori.org/training/

This website gives details of the official teacher training diploma and other courses for teachers wishing to embed Maria Montessori's child-centred values in their classroom.

http://www.steinerwaldorf.org/steiner-teachers/teacher-education

This website gives details and links to teacher training courses offered in the UK and Ireland for teachers at Steiner-Waldorf schools and for teachers based in mainstream schools who wish to deepen and develop their existing practices.

http://www.holisticeducationuk.org/holisticteachertraining/

The Holistic Education Organisation provides a useful selection of links to teacher training or retraining programmes which promote more holistic approaches to education.

Appendix 3: books and articles

In this section, we have selected some books and articles which can help to enrich our understanding and appreciation of HCE. None of these texts directly conceptualise education and learning from a human-centred perspective. However, they are meaningful in enabling us to critique a certain malaise in the educational system, such as coercion, a narrow focus on high-stakes testing performance, instrumentalisation of education, and so on, and at the same time they help us to see the potential and possibilities of taking a humanising and human-centred approach in transforming education.

Achacoso, M. & Svinicki, M. (eds.). (2004). *Alternative strategies for evaluating student learning*. San Francisco, CA: Jossey-Bass Publishers.
This book contains some good examples that illustrate non-tests-based evaluative practice, some of which provide learning feedback to students, others offering evaluation in accordance to a set of criteria or recognised standards. Although most strategies are applied within further and higher education contexts, many of the ideas could be applied in secondary education.

Ben-Ze'ev, A. (2000). *The subtlety of emotions*. Cambridge, MA: The MIT Press.
This book offers an overall conceptual framework for conceptualising emotions and for discussing different individual emotions and exploring the landscape of human affective experiences. This is a helpful text for us to understand the relationship between emotions and motivation.

Black, P. & Wiliam, D. (1998). *Inside the black box*. London: King's College.
This book critiques classroom practice using the metaphor of the black box where inputs from outside (teachers, teaching, resources, parental pressure, test scores) might result in outputs (knowledge, skills and competencies). The authors propose that assessment should be an integral part of learning and in so conceiving, teaching involves ongoing feedback to the students' work. This is termed 'formative assessment' and later, 'assessment for learning'. This book is helpful to understand the challenge within mainstream education to practise non-judgemental and integrated learning.

Booth, T. (2011). Curricula for the common school: What shall we tell our children? *Forum*, *53*(1), pp. 31–48.
In this article, the author reflects on the way in which curriculum has been conceived in the past and present, and suggests that curriculum must build from experience, be values- and rights-based and, therefore, inclusive. Proposals include making learning relevant to the students' and community's life, engaging with pressing local and global topics such as sustainability and locating our lives in the past, present and future. This article helps us to rethink the structure of curriculum.

Dewey, J. (1938). *Experience and education*. New York: Collier Books.
This is a classic text which remains relevant today, especially in the way it articulates the importance for students to connect to the purpose of education and learning, the necessity to incorporate experience in the process of learning which in turn is to be directed by the teachers, and the need to encourage the student's freedom of intelligence which consists in the power to frame the objectives, evaluate one's desires and wants, and have time and space for observing, thinking and reflecting.

Fielding, M. (2006). Leadership, radical student engagement and the necessity of person-centred education. *International Journal of Leadership in Education,* 9(4), pp. 299–313.
In this article, Fielding sets out a four-fold typology of the interpersonal orientation of schools as organisations/communities, from impersonal, affective, high performance, to person-centred modes of being. In particular, he explains that schools must be person-centred learning communities permeated by personal (as opposed to functional) relationships. This text is most helpful in enabling us to understand the imperative of developing human-centred learning communities in education.

Fielding, M. & Moss, P. (2010). *Radical education and the common schools: A democratic alternative.* Oxford: Routledge.
This book claims to offer a 'fundamentally redesigned but pragmatically possible alternative for education and schooling' (p. 2), using the Reggio Emilia approach and St George-in-the-East School's pedagogy to illustrate such possibilities at primary and secondary levels respectively. The St George example is highly relevant to the human-centred approach discussed in this handbook.

Forbes, S. (2003). *Holistic education: An analysis of its ideas and nature.* Brandon, VT: Foundation for Educational Renewal.
This book explores some of the philosophical influences, including Rousseau, Pestalozzi, Froebel, Jung, Maslow and Rogers, behind the idea of holistic education and attributes it to the notion of 'ultimacy', which points to the aim of education as enabling greater connectedness, a harmony between the inner and outer life (if these can be distinguished so) and reaching the highest potential possible. This book helps us to consider the importance of whole-person development through education.

Freire, P. (1970). *Pedagogy of the oppressed.* New York: Seabury Press.
The most important concept put forward by this book is the idea that the aim of education is to enable us to become more fully human. In contrast to a 'banking' approach to education and schooling that tend to dehumanise both students and the teachers, Freire proposes a dialogic pedagogy where the individual becomes more aware of one's imcompleteness and limited situations, and that through mutual humanisation, education serves to transform the human's ways of being and the world at large. This text supports the aims of education as identified by the human-centred approach.

Gergen, K. (2009). *Relational being: Beyond self and community.* New York: Oxford University Press.
This book articulates clearly a vision of relational being, where meaning derives from coordinated action and all that we hold as meaningful and valuable depends on the richness of our relationships. In particular, the author highlights ways to go about education in a relational way.

Gill, S. & Thomson, G. (2012). *Rethinking secondary education: A human-centred approach.* London: Pearson Education.
Our book discusses a human-centred approach to curriculum, pedagogy, assessment and the culture of schools and colleges. It is grounded in theoretical exploration and empirical research, highlighting the need for a curriculum for the future, bridging a gap between mainstream and alternative education and presenting a hopeful picture for educational transformation. The book not only offers a robust theoretical grounding on the key concepts of HCE, but also takes a balanced approach, comparing and contrasting both traditional and alternative approaches to education, enriching the research with the inclusion of young people's perspectives and 'voices' on their education and on the challenges faced and lived by adolescents. It is an ideal companion for this handbook.

Gill, S. & Thomson, G. (Eds.). (2014). *Redefining religious education: Spirituality for human flourishing*. New York: Palgrave Macmillan.
This book is a unique collection of interdisciplinary articles that argue for religious education to be directed primarily towards the spiritual insofar as it is part of a flourishing human life. The articles address this issue from the perspectives of theory, different religious traditions and innovative teaching and learning practices. These are meaningful texts to support whole-person education and locate spirituality within HCE. This book complements our book on HCE.

Gribble, D. (1998). *Real education: varieties of freedom*. Bristol: Libertarian Education.
This book includes interesting examples of alternative schools from around the world that exhibit some aspects relevant to HCE, such as the human-scale environment, priority of relationships, respect and attention to the students' interests and needs, a focus on cultivating students' responsibilities for learning and personal development, and balancing social, emotional and creative aspects and the academic.

Holt, J. (1964). *How children fail*. New York: Pitman Press.
This is another classic text in which Holt objects to the coercive and highly pressurised educational culture and the suppression of the students' intrinsic motivation in mainstream education. Instead, he promotes freedom to learn, rich and stimulating learning environments, tuning students' readiness to learn, fostering students' autonomy and responsibility, space to identify and follow one's own interests, and making available rich resources. It articulates clearly how and why traditional schooling ensures that children will fail their education, and how by respecting the students and their needs, education will move away from teaching subjects towards teaching human.

Hubbard, B. (2008). Beyond tests and quizzes: Creative assessments in the college classroom. *Community College Journal of Research and Practice*, 32, pp. 730–735.
This article contrasts the standardised testing with the real purpose of evaluation, which is providing feedback to both students and teachers for improvement. Some of the ideas in terms of how teachers could do the latter are creative and plausible. In particular, it proposes that any evaluative practices mustn't be detached from the nature of the tasks.

Krishnamurti, J. (2008). *Education and the significance of life*. London: HarperCollins.
The book problematises conformity and loss of personal values as the result of traditional education, which is the root of the mounting destruction and misery. Instead, education's purpose is seen as cultivating self-understanding through being present in oneself and being able to discern and engage with one's emotional states. Themes covered in this book include authority versus freedom, discipline, intelligence, and the role of religion in education. It is a sound critique of the traditional schooling model.

Bennett, B., Cunningham, I. & Dawes, G. (2000). *Self managed learning in action: Putting SML into practice*. England: Gower.
Although written in the contexts of organisations and organisational learning, this book captures the essence of self-managed learning and how to structure a self-managed learning programme in an organisation. This could be used as a reference if schools are interested in using this approach, especially in the way the three key elements of learning group, learning agreement and learning community are integrated in the mentoring sessions and group sessions.

Macmurray, J. (2012). Learning to be human. *Oxford Review of Education* 38(6), pp. 661–674.
In this reprint of Macmurray's 1958 lecture, the author argues for a deeply relational nature of human's being and insists that the fundamental aim of education is for us to learn to be human, with one another. In particular, Macmurray stresses the inescapable necessity of

personal relations (as opposed to functional) between teachers and students and the quality of education rests on the quality of this relation. This is one of the key texts that lays the foundation for relationally enriched and enriching education and is particularly

Marples, R. (Ed.). (1999). *The aims of education*. London: Routledge.
This edited volume consists of twelve chapters offered by Western philosophers of education, each exploring and questioning from the diverse strains of the liberal tradition the aims of education (including autonomy, fairness, well-being, moral seriousness, social commitment, critical thinking and self-determination) and other key issues such as identity, curriculum and pedagogy. These texts are meaningful in informing us about the different arguments of the aims and purposes of education.

Neill, A. S. (1992). *Summerhill School: A new view of childhood*. New York: St. Martin's Griffin.
This book suggests that emotions (not intellect) are the primary driving forces that shape a young person's growth, and offers a radical example of schooling of Summerhill, which is a self-governing democratic learning community. It allows us to see what happens to the young people and their learning when decisions and responsibilities are left entirely to them.

Noddings, N. (2003). *Happiness and education*. Cambridge, MA: University Press.
Here is another book that explores the aims of education. Noddings discusses what happiness means, in both personal and public domains. In her exploration, the notion of happiness to some extent resembles our conception of flourishing. However, what is most relevant for us is her elaboration on happiness as an aim of education, what education would look at in terms of relationships, curriculum and pedagogy, and the lenses we take to evaluate education.

Palmer, P. (2004). *A hidden wholeness: The journey toward an undivided life*. San Francisco, CA: Jossey-Bass.
In this book, Palmer explores what it means to pursue an integral life (the inner and outer), the meaning of community, teaching and learning for transformation, and non-violent social change. An important proposal made in this book is the need to create 'circles of trust' for teachers to engage in self-transformation, mutual healing and renewal – a real sense of being in communion. This book highlights the necessity of teachers' whole-person development as the basis for developing whole-person pedagogy.

Pye, J. (1989). *Invisible children: Who are the real losers at school?* Oxford: Oxford Paperbacks.
This book provides an account of the plight of 'invisible' students who offer neither challenge nor difficulty to their teachers and therefore pass through their schooling largely unnoticed, a shortcoming of secondary education in modern Britain. The author questions whether relationships between the teacher and the students are possible in an overly crowded secondary class, and what constraints teachers must overcome in order to reach all students.

Pring, R. (2013). *The life and death of secondary education for all*. Oxford: Routledge.
This book contains philosophical analysis as well as empirical illustrations on what makes a meaningful secondary education for the sake of the positive learning experiences of young people. It discusses more specifically the curriculum, the work and training of teachers, the evaluative criteria in terms of how well it has worked, some proposed frameworks for qualification and so on. Once again, what is most relevant to our concern is the further exploration of the aim of education, this time from the perspective of 'education for all'.

Zubizarreta, J. (2009). *The learning portfolio: Reflective practice for improving student learning*. San Francisco, CA: Jossey-Bass Publishers.

This book offers diverse ways to document students' work. Despite the fact that the portfolio ideas collected in the book are generally limited to intellectual or academic work, these grounded samples are nonetheless meaningful in exhibiting the value of reflective practices about learning and how criteria for standards and rubrics for evaluation can be applied in gathering and reviewing the portfolios. Some are refreshing ideas to try out when considering using portfolios as part of the human-centred approach to learning feedback, review and evaluation.

Bibliography

Bernstein, B. (1977). *Class codes and control. Vol 3, Towards a theory of educational transmissions.* London: Routledge and Kegan Paul.

Bernstein, B. (1990). *The structuring of pedagogic discourse.* London: Routledge.

Cooperrider, D. L. & Whitney, D. (2005). *Appreciative inquiry: A positive revolution in change.* San Francisco, CA: Berrett-Koehler Publishers.

Fielding, M. (2014). Radical democratic education as response to two world wars and a contribution to world peace: The inspirational work of Alex Bloom. *Forum, 56*(3), pp. 513–528.

Fielding, M. (2005). Alex Bloom, pioneer of radical state education, *Forum, 47*(2), pp. 119–134.

Gill, S. & Thomson, G. (2012). *Rethinking Secondary education: A human-centred approach.* London: Pearson Education.

Gill, S. & Goodson, I. (2001). *Narrative pedagogy.* New York: Peter Lang.

Macmurray, J. (1961). *Reason and emotion.* London: Faber & Faber.

Robbins, A. (1995). *Notes from a friend: A quick and simple guide to taking charge of your life.* London: Simon & Schuster Ltd.

Index